KNOW YOUR STYLE

MIX IT, MATCH IT, LOVE IT

ALYSON WALSH

KNOW YOUR STYLE

MIX IT, MATCH IT, LOVE IT

ARTWORK BY AYUMI TAKAHASHI

hardie grant books

Introduction

What does 'know your style' even mean? Is it akin to knowing yourself, or knowing your onions – or perhaps a bit of both? Over my 30-year career in fashion, from magazine reader makeovers to meeting women at various events and online, or simply chatting to friends (even the ones who seem confident, comfortable and chic), I have regularly been asked questions about style. And this often comes down to establishing 'what goes with what'. Which accessories complement a favourite outfit, which colours coordinate well – or make the perfect mismatch – what to wear for a special occasion without spending loads of money or ending up looking like Barbara Cartland?

Knowing what goes with what does involve an element of gut instinct, but I do think style is something that can be learned. You can practise it. I mentioned this phenomenon to author and former magazine editor Maggie Alderson, who recalls how much she loved watching the transformation of young fashion assistants during her stint at *Elle* magazine (like a more benign version of *The Devil Wears Prada*). Young women would appear on their first day in a new Topshop outfit and then gradually develop a more individual look by adding a Calvin Klein bias-cut dress here, a pair of sneakers there...

'I think great style is individuality with confidence,' Lucinda Chambers, fashion director at British *Vogue*, tells me, 'I don't think it has to be chic or elegant, it just has to be authentic to you and a little bit different.' Thankfully, the social media age – as well as age in general – has removed the need to follow trends. There's more freedom today and fewer rigid style rules. We lead busy lives, requiring more ease and simplicity and less of the faff factor (see page 20).

It's important to embrace considerate consumption and avoid fast fashion; I practise the one-in-one-out rule and always donate unwanted clothes to charity. I tend to buy things I love and wear them until they fall apart. As Anna Garner, a former fashion director at Selfridges and Henri Bendel's and now founder of *thegarnered.com*, concurs, 'It's not about price, it's about quality and buying better. Style can be wearing something that's 30 years old and making it look great. I love an item that's a little bit eclectic, that can make an outfit belong to that person.'

There are many ways to know your style, as the numerous experts I interviewed for this book show. Whether personal style involves having a formula or a uniform, or taking a more eclectic approach, it's always important to know what suits in terms of body shape, lifestyle and personality. If you know your style, you know that when you put something on in the morning, you have the confidence to carry it off and feel comfortable for the rest of the day. Style is personal – celebrate individuality and do your thing.

Style —
you can
practise it!

DO TRY THIS AT HOME

We happily spend time preparing food and perfecting recipes, fine-tuning a yoga move or musical performance, but when it comes to clothes and putting outfits together, there is definitely a more devil-may-care tendency to throw things on and hope for the best. A tried-and-tested recipe is something we come back to; once accomplished, confidence allows us to experiment with new ingredients, to jazz things up and add a bit of ourselves. The idea of practising style, of working at what we wear until it's perfect, is so obvious, yet rarely undertaken.

'Style is different to taste. It is a very personal expression. Taste is built up from what you love, your cultural and design references, things you keep close to you... the tools you use to define your personality. Style is how you reflect your personality, the little touches on an outfit, how you might tie your belt or scarf... what you want your message to the world to be.'

-

Caroline Issa
Chief executive and fashion director at *Tank* magazine

Several women I spoke to while researching this book admitted that they had been doing their homework and thinking about 'what goes with what'; making calculations, considering different combinations of clothes, figuring out the outfits that work, as well as the absolute no-nos. Amelia Bullmore, the actor and writer, had thrown her clothes onto the bedroom floor to get a good overview and then handpicked bits and pieces from there. Sarah Arnett, illustrator and textile designer, had drawn her outfits every day to try to work out if there was a pattern. But I think Lucinda Chambers, fashion director at British *Vogue*, nailed it when she said, 'The most stylish women I know are older – one is in her eighties and the other in her sixties. I think it takes time, and that's all right. I can't be doing with the idea that "you are born with style". That's nonsense; you should experiment and play around and make mistakes because it will get easier if you practise!' Not everyone has Chambers' outstanding natural ability, but we can all practise.

This involves taking time to think, plan, coordinate or contrast. Time is the modern-day luxury we never have enough of, but I've decided to put the smartphone down every once in a while and give myself a bit of space. Setting aside an afternoon, once a season – or at least getting up earlier once a week to have a play around – not only makes sense, it makes getting dressed easier and provides more options.

'When I wake up in the morning I lie in bed for 15 minutes thinking about what I should wear,' confesses Sarah Arnett, who wears a different outfit every day. 'I've learnt that spending an afternoon trying on clothes isn't an indulgence, it's part of my job. It makes me understand things.' And understanding things, from the colours that go together and suit your complexion to the silhouettes that work for your body shape, so that you know what you're looking for when you go shopping, is paramount.

'What are we doing when we put things on, take them off, put them on, take them off? You could call this feminine chaos or you could call it practising,' adds Amelia Bullmore. 'Don't tell me Anita Ekberg got it right the first time...' Bullmore admits that practising is a lifelong hobby she started as a teenager, and that she keeps a notebook for writing down 'good combos'. Bullmore continues, 'Sometimes, when my husband Paul is away or I'm at home on my own in the evening, I'll be messing about trying clothes on. I'm embarrassed to tell people because they'll think it's a mad, vain pursuit.'

From architects to curators to knitwear designers, all the women I interviewed had one thing in common: they spend time organising and refining their work. We all do. Admittedly, there is a natural talent, an instinct involved. 'I guess one can get better,' says Linda Rodin, fashion stylist, beauty entrepreneur and model, 'and with "practice" one can get good at putting things together, but never with the flair and ease of someone who "has it" in their blood. Practice, of course, improves the skill, but not the finesse, or the art.' True. Some of us are good at employment law or accounting, others work in creative industries as stylists, designers or directors. And with creativity there is a little magic and mystery involved, which is virtually impossible to explain (believe me, I've tried), but Chambers has a go: 'It sounds pretentious, but colours speak to me. It's a voice, a physical reaction to two pieces that work together. You almost want to get it wrong so that you can get it right.'

Practising can be as much about what doesn't work as what does. Putting things on and then taking them off again in front of a full-length mirror; figuring out what looks best, what makes you feel good and what makes you look like you got dressed in the dark. Chambers says, 'I just keep putting things on, keep adding, so that it's full of colour – not shoving it all on, but building up to a styling sensation. If it's too much, take it off.'

'It is helpful to have a uniform,' continues Chambers, 'to invest money in a beautifully tailored pair of black trousers, a pinstriped men's shirt and a gilet coat. Having a uniform can give you confidence. If you haven't got confidence, then get a uniform and you don't have to think about it. Then, after a while, you might want to branch out a bit and focus on statement shoes or earrings or a necklace.' Back to the

example of the winning recipe, this is like the no-brainer pasta dish pulled out on a Saturday night and livened up with a few new ingredients bought at the local market earlier in the day.

And, when an outfit works, keep wearing it. With this in mind, I was relieved to learn that, like myself, many women often wear the same clothes two or three days in a row (heatwaves excluded). This is not complacency, it's common sense. 'I have a lot of shoes,' says Rodin. 'I could wear the same outfit four days in a row and just change the shoes. You can change the whole look with a different colour shoe, a bootie or a sneaker. I do the same thing with coats in winter.' As with leftovers, outfits are better the next day. Which is even more satisfying because you don't have to put as much effort in. Often the clothes are multiples, so there's nothing slovenly about this two-day style trip. Or the second layer remains the same but everything underneath is fresh; for example, I'll wear the same jeans and sweater for a few days on the trot, but my underwear is clean and so is my long-sleeved T-shirt. On the second day, the accessories are different – I've swapped silver hoops for statement earrings and my hair is tied up – or, like Rodin, I'll add a different coat or pair of shoes.

At an impromptu styling session with Bullmore, she agreed to throw her clothes on the floor for me (I still have the photos on my phone). I was struck by Bullmore's prudence. There were no rails of fancy stuff; it was all

'It's the mixing and the layering. I do really like layers. I'll wear two tailored jackets or two cardigans – say, a small tailored jacket with a great big cashmere cardigan over the top.'

-

Amy de la Haye
Dress historian, curator, author and professor at London College of Fashion

very discreet and low-key and a lot of the clothes were quite old. And that's the thing. Style doesn't equal buying loads of new stuff; endless consumerism doesn't make anyone happy – or stylish. This is the age of shopping for your lifestyle and not just for the sake of it. These are the buy less, buy better years. My friend, the knitwear designer Jo Gordon, describes this phenomenon as 'penny-a-day clothing'. If it's expensive and you wear it a lot and have it for years, it ends up costing a penny a day. I'm not saying experts don't matter. They do. In Chapter 6, No more wardrobe chaos (see page 128), I have a session with a wardrobe consultant and this editing and prioritising not only helped me to see what I had more clearly, but it helped me look at the bigger picture, too. My wardrobe was energised, not by going and buying new things, but by laying the foundations for the future. What I have to work with are some good-quality not-so-basic basics; to these, I will add regular, seasonal updates – the latest denim

silhouette or cocktail sneakers, a super shirt in a fresh colour, a new silk scarf – little touches to liven things up.

Style is individual – and traditional, prescriptive rules are no longer relevant. There are many ways to dress and different pairings work for different individuals. Your body is your design brief, so be honest with yourself about what works and what doesn't. Spend time working out different combinations of clothes that fit and flatter and create a handful of go-to outfits that allow you to whip up a styling sensation. And carry on experimenting. I love finding a new winning combination. The navy, jersey, pussy-bow top unlocked by my 10-year-old Marc by Marc Jacobs navy-and-black patterned jacket and old Levi's 501s. Result. Once the basics are in place, then the fun begins. As Chambers points out, 'It has to have authenticity. You've got to believe in it. You have to have integrity; you're not putting it on for personal effect, you're putting it on for pleasure.'

How to practise style cheat sheet

Kim Winser, CEO and founder of British womenswear brand Winser London, gives her expert advice on practising style.

Stick to what suits

I'm tall (5 ft 10 in/1.78 m), bigger on the top and slimmer on the hips, so I dress for my figure. For people to become confident with their proportions, this is something that I think is so important. We all have good things – it could be strong shoulders or a great waist, it can be anything – and we should celebrate that.

Wear new combinations of old favourites

I travel regularly and wear a lot of the same things, differently. I'll wear an English-made tweed coat in black or ivory to a board meeting, and in the evening I'll dress it up with a silk pussybow tunic blouse. Sometimes I undo the silk blouse and loosen it so that it comes down to the knee and looks more relaxed. I tend to switch trousers around, so I'll wear leggings and suede Saint Laurent boots, or tapered trousers with Prada skate shoes, and keep the tweed coat and silk blouse. I'm wearing the same things, but my outfits look different because I've put them together in a fresh way.

Personal style should evolve

I'm always challenging myself: in life, in business and in what I wear. My style has evolved but I realise it's a work in progress. After years in the boardroom I wasn't sure about wearing a more casual tapered trouser such as a jogger at first, but they work, and now I'll wear them on a flight or in a meeting.

'Last year I made the decision not to buy any new clothes. Just to buy second-hand or to revamp what I already have. I've had this beautiful satin dress for a very long time – the colours are quite dirty: rusty brown, pink, silver, pale blue and hints of blood red – but I hardly wore it until recently. Then I bought a pair of pale pink brothel creepers for 25 quid on eBay and now I feel that I can absolutely wear it during the day and not feel overdressed.'

-

Sarah Arnett
Textile designer

HOW TO AVOID THE FAFF FACTOR

Often avoidable, faffing can be instigated by external circumstances (weather fluctuations, commuting on a steaming hot train) as well as impractical clothing or a poor fit. The result is unnecessary discomfort, frustration and even more faffage: it's a vicious circle. Clothes with a high faff factor include: tights (pantyhose) that aren't long enough so the crotch ends up at the knees, bra straps that constantly fall off the shoulders and items made from poor-quality fabrics. All of which can lead to a chic meltdown – which has nothing to do with freakin' out to *Le Freak* at a friend's house party... Here are three easy ways to eliminate the faff factor (I know, I've practised).

1. Buy clothes that fit

Fit is everything. If it doesn't sit right, it doesn't fit right and is going to be bothersome. 'Comfort is greatly underrated,' comments Lucinda Chambers, fashion director at British *Vogue*, 'I don't think anyone can be "stylish" if a) the clothes don't fit or b) for any reason you feel uncomfortable in them. They just won't work.' Good fit = less faff. End of.

2. Be prepared (for the weather)

On one of those steamy, stormy summer days in London when the weather feels like it's blown straight in from the Indian Ocean, I interviewed Marie Wilkinson of Cutler and Gross. The design director turned up in a transparent rubberised rain mac (with hood) from Margaret Howell, statement glasses, strong lipstick, culottes and Tracey Neuls water-resistant Geek shoes. No tidemarks, damp patches or rain-sodden hems; just perfectly composed and prepared for the elements. I was impressed. Whether you're commuting, socialising or glamping, staying dry equates with staying chic. As Alfred Wainwright said, 'There is no such thing as bad weather, only unsuitable clothing.' Conversely, staying stylish in a heatwave doesn't mean wearing last year's holiday clothes. Looser fitting clothes in natural fabrics – wide-leg linen trousers and a silk shell top, jersey harem pants with an oversized cotton shirt – stay cool and provide a little waft factor. And if that doesn't work, acquire a gran fan (battery operated/hand-held) – available from Muji.

3. Wear big undies and the right bra

My bra history goes like this: young, flat-chested and embarrassed, I would guess my size and grab the first bra I could find, rather than actually seeking advice or trying anything on. Older, saggier and less concerned about what other people think, I'm more inclined to loiter in underwear departments, demanding attention and feeding my expensive lingerie habit. I'm wondering if there is a correlation?

As confidence and earnings go up, nipples head in the opposite direction. I'm not going to bang on about bras, but breasts change throughout our lives – particularly after pregnancy and menopause – so bras need to be regularly fitted and provide enough support to avoid navel grazing.

And thank God, the thong is long gone. I never really understood its appeal. Give me big panties any day of the week. Sizeable, stretch-cotton undies are cool and comfy; there's no VPL, chafing or hitching and hoicking. Much better than briefs that are so brief you end up chewing cloth.

Where to find them: Standard Drawers, Figleaves, Baserange, Gap Body, Hanro, Muji, M&S, Bravissimo, & Other Stories.

Mastering contrast and colour

IT'S ALL ABOUT
THE CONTRAST

What the Italians call *spezzato* – a gentle juxtaposition of contrasting items – makes the essentials look extraordinary. As Lisa Salzer, founder of Lulu Frost, so brilliantly puts it, 'Matchy-matchy is over. Unless you're going to a fancy dress party as Nancy Reagan.' Coordinating accessories to outfits does feel very last century, very formal. Even the British royal family has moved on (apart from the Queen, but she is 90-odd). Dressing today is all about contrast. 'You've got to take risks and not be afraid of experimentation,' continues Salzer, 'not assume that rules from the past apply any more.'

'I'm a quirky
dresser – I love to mix
colour and layer.
I suppose boho chic is
in my gut, but then I also
love a beautifully cut
pair of navy trousers
and a navy shirt;
there's nothing nicer
than navy if you want
to look really
chic and glamorous.'

-

Pandora Delevigne
Personal stylist

Silhouettes, colours, patterns, textures, accessories; contrast means pairing two mismatching items together – placing velvet with denim or sneakers with a trouser suit. Dress codes may be looser, but this is not about casually throwing items on; the aim is to look effortless and pulled-together.

Take time to try out new combinations and avoid looking like you got dressed blindfolded. Here are some tips to get it right:

Try opposing textures

Blend colourful tweed with a slinky silk blouse. Mix military and metallic – wear an army jacket and a sequined skirt. Team leather leggings with a slouchy cashmere sweater. Going for a mismatch keeps it modern.

Play with pattern

Balance different proportions: a narrow black-and-white striped shirt with a wider-striped trouser (pair of pants). Wear a leopard-print coat over a vintage floral dress. Mix a Missoni zigzag with a Breton stripe.

Shape shift your silhouette

Try a shirt with big trumpet sleeves and a form-fitting pencil skirt. Merge a Mitford-esque posh cocktail frock with a mannish tuxedo jacket. Shape up in a cocoon coat and slim-leg pants.

Combine cool colours

Go for a clash-up with a pink tuxedo and a small red cross-body bag. Wear a pair of mustard trousers and a petrol-blue sweater. Fall for a forest-green coat and a burnt-orange dress. Make it an artful combination.

It takes knitwear designer Jo Gordon six weeks to work out new colour combinations, every season. Known for her singular, often stripy vision, she uses pattern and colour to create outstanding accessories. One thing I am interested to find out is how Gordon works out what goes with what. 'I have lots of recipes in my head. It's like a creative affliction!' she says. 'I know what kind of blue goes with what kind of yellow, but this can change. My mum was a painter and talked a lot about colour; it obviously sank in.'

At her south London studio, simple patterns are created by computer, but the more complex designs and special one-offs are mocked-up on paper. I'm delighted, on my visit, when Gordon rolls out a strip of paper the size of a scarf with all the different colours stuck on it; like 2D Tom Baker neckwear. Colour swatches are laid out on a table by the window, under a daylight bulb, where Gordon experiments with different combinations. When I ask how she works it all out, she says, 'It's something I do every day, but it's hard to put into words. My primary interest is composition of colour and I am constantly playing around and putting colours together until something clicks.'

Juxtaposing bolds and neutrals is a Jo Gordon thing. Looking closely at her stripy knits, I pick out the following: a dirty duck-egg blue and a flame orange sitting next to a charcoal grey; an egg-yolk yellow next to a blueish-green and a flannel grey; and an emerald green and a scarlet sitting by a subtle brown-y colour. 'I like colours that live dangerously next to each other,' she continues. 'Colours that look quite surprising together, but sit nicely, like green and pink. They look great together within a garment, but I wouldn't want to wear just those two colours. I think bright colours work best when they are in the midst of lots of interesting neutrals. Then they really sing out.'

Gordon's inspiration comes not from fashion trends but from everyday items. 'I take photos throughout the year; I'm always seeing great colour combinations.' She admits, 'It may be what someone's wearing on the street, the blue-and-yellow paintwork at Peckham Rye train station or a plate of colourful food. We are selling in winter and so I do think about what will look good with winter coats. Pale colours don't sell well and my preference is for stronger tones anyway.'

The accessory brings all Gordon's own clothes to life, 'My clothes are pretty neutral: black, denim, Prussian blue, but then I will wear a really fantastic wrap. I'd love more time to make decisions about what to wear – my 16-year-old daughter wears pattern-upon-pattern; she has a very clever knack of teaming clashing patterns together.' I ask her if there are any colours she wouldn't work with (or wear). 'I have to say I rarely go to the purple range on my colour charts. I am very anti-purple and lilac. I get that from my mum – she hated it. But the weirdest thing was that she turned up in lilac-purple

Jean Muir at my wedding and looked absolutely fantastic. So I guess I should never say never.'

Gordon has some great advice on choosing colours to wear: 'Do it slowly. Pick your colours carefully. You have to be comfortable that you look good in what you're wearing. If you find it difficult, start with a little neckerchief and move on to something more adventurous.' To determine if it suits you, she suggests holding the garment up to your face, 'to see whether your skin lights up and looks healthy, or if it pulls the colour out of your face. I used to wear a lot more black – and still wear old, black items that have faded – but I wear a lot more Prussian blue (a dark, inky blueish-black). If I'm feeling pale and pasty, it really lifts me.' This can change from season to season: 'There is no formula, no rules – spend time looking and seeing, understand what you look good in – and that can mean different colours at different times of the year. Make time to play around and experiment, to decide what works for you.' She concludes: 'Only wear clothes that make you feel great. I only buy an item of clothing if it immediately makes me feel fantastic when I try it on.'

Some of my favourite colourful brands:
Daniela Gregis, Toast, Paul Smith, Dries Van Noten,
Jospeh, COS, Roksanda, Hobbs, Gudrun Sjoden.

Three women explain how to introduce a new hue:

Start with a blank canvas

'My clothes are mainly black and I use a white shirt like a canvas,' proclaims professor Lyn Slater. Known for creating a visually arresting outfit from a largely neutral palette, Slater prefers to keep colour to a minimum. 'I have worn pink, grey and navy but I think the rest of the colour world is out. I don't think it's flattering to me – colour as an accent is much more exciting.'

Be inspired by nature

Whether at the beach, sitting in the park or halfway up a mountain, natural surroundings tend to calm and complement, rather than jar. 'I have a thing about pinks and greens together, and blue and brown together,' says footwear designer Penelope Chilvers. 'Analysing why makes me realise these are the colours of nature. I'm quite outdoorsy and so I like to see these colours and textures together.'

Consider a colour reboot

Throughout our lives, both hair colour and skin tone change, and may necessitate a style reboot. 'Now I've gone blonde, grey, black, white and paler, slightly underwear-y colours look great,' points out actor and writer Amelia Bullmore, 'You've just got to keep trying things, look at it and think, "Is that good?", put something else on and think, "Is that better?"'

'It's all about a great combination: old/new, expensive/inexpensive, charity shops/designer, good bits/faded bits. I like things that go against each other, the texture and shape – so I'll wear a Lurex jumper with a pair of school trousers. I'll put an opulent texture with a practical texture.'

-

Amelia Bullmore
Actor and writer

WEARING PATTERN AND PRINT

I like pattern and print when I see it on other objects, like art-gallery walls, soft furnishings and ceramics, but not so much on me. On a scale of surface decoration (a pie chart of pattern?), I definitely gravitate towards the plain end; but I love a good Liberty print, a vintage paisley or a Josef Frank textile design from Svenskt Tenn. I'm fine with leopard print, camouflage and all kinds of stripes, but there's just something about bigger, bolder, more colourful prints that makes me feel quite self-conscious. Yet bold pattern in fashion can look fantastic: I'm thinking Rosita Missoni, Iris Apfel, Stella Jean. How do you make a statement and look considered when pattern-wearing? I'll pass that one over to illustrator and textile designer Sarah Arnett...

'I think it's the colour combination that rules over everything else. Mixing pattern and wearing pattern really works when the colours work. This week I'm wearing a bright-blue patterned shirt with a slim, black V-neck sweater and a red patterned African-print cotton jacket over the top. I'll wear this with black jeans. This outfit has a consideration to it and so I don't feel messy.

'Wear something to make space between the prints. So a belt or an element – like my black jumper – that separates the prints. If you wear lots of colour and pattern and don't have something to break it up, you feel a bit upholstered. Breaking the colour up makes it feel like you're wearing clothes.

'Pattern can be used as a kind of cover-up – don't look at me, look at the pattern! With the boldness of print, you definitely won't go unnoticed, but breaking it up differentiates parts of an outfit. Have a narrative. Arrange the clothes and work out the different combinations of patterns – though, having said that, it's also lovely when you try something on and it works in an unexpected way. This happens when you buy clothes; you have an idea about wearing something in one way but end up wearing it another. I guess the more interesting outcome is that you don't have to follow rules. It's quite exciting.

'It takes a bit of effort, a lot of trying on. I spend hours trying things on – or I'll cut up a dress and play around with it until it works. I could make any dress or print that I want, but sometimes I still don't know what to wear. It takes practice. You're changing all the time, getting older, wanting different things. You have to keep practising.'

'I don't wear pastels,
I wish I could wear
dusky pink, but it doesn't
really work with
my skin colour.
It looks a bit saccharine.
The colours I wear
tend to be stronger
and richer.'

Nimi Attanayake
Architect and RIBA ambassador

LUCINDA CHAMBERS

Colour, print and texture... I love all of those and if I find something, usually vintage, that has all three, then I can get overexcited. It's not because designers now don't embrace those things – they do and it's wonderful, but I think I tend to buy plainer things from contemporary designers so that I don't see them so much everywhere. I guess I'm a bit of a snob like that. I like my clothes not to be easily identifiable. But I am as happy in the high street as I am with designer clothes; in fact, I am happiest when I mix the two and then throw vintage in. It sounds very deliberate and hard work, but I don't think it through like that.

I have a pretty eclectic taste. It's very diverse. I always have big khaki trousers and a stripy T-shirt, but I have a cull every few years. I wear ankle socks a lot with high heels or big shoes – that's a signature thing that I do. I don't wear tights (pantyhose), but I buy socks whenever I see them from Tabio and COS, and & Other Stories has an unexpectedly full range.

Everything matched when I was at school and college, and it was usually purple. Purple eyeshadow, with a purple dress and earrings – I must have looked very odd. I loved clothes, but, thinking about it, I didn't know how to find how I wanted to look.

I love tinkering around with clothes and I guess I dress decoratively. I'm very nostalgic about old things. And if I have just bought something, and have put it together with an old, faded, rosy slip dress or pair of pyjama trousers and the two seem to say hello to each other, I will be excited by that.

I know what I like and I want to achieve a couple of things. One is that I want to feel excited by what I wear and I want other people to feel braver about what they wear, but I want to feel appropriate, too. Oddly, I don't want to stand out, I just want to make the best of myself.

Fashion director at British *Vogue*

NIMI ATTANAYAKE

'Architects tend to wear black, but I think, if you're representing a business, you have to be memorable in some way. I like outfits that are quite rich.

My favourite is a brilliantlly colourful Marimekko dress that I usually wear with bright yellow sandals from Camper and white, mirrored Ray-Ban sunglasses. I'll probably add some punchy nail varnish (I like 623 Mirabella by Chanel). It's a summer dress in a lightweight cotton, with a gathered round neck and a matching fabric tie-belt, which falls just above the knee. The shape is simple, but the detail has been considered. The colour and pattern (white, blue, pink, yellow and red abstract) is fun and always makes me feel happy. It reminds me not to take fashion (and possibly life) too seriously and that both can be playful as well as formal. Also, it's a tunic dress, so I don't feel constricted or body-conscious when I wear it.

It's quite precious to my heart and so I don't want to wear it too often. I wore it last year for a good friend's wedding in the sunny English countryside and it fitted right in. Since buying it I have developed an expensive obsession with all things Marimekko and I now have a lot of their dresses. My mum's a bit of a hoarder and I think I'm following in her footsteps. I have 20 pieces of Marimekko clothing. It started with dresses – now I've moved on to tights, skirts, Converse, homeware… Sometimes the mug matches the dress. This could end up in a really bad place!

I'm short and pear-shaped. My style is eclectic and, at times, bold. I think because my husband and I are quite small, colour makes us feel a bit bigger. I haven't always dressed this way. I think as I mature and understand myself more, my fashion sense has become focussed and taken shape.

Architect and RIBA ambassador '

Living a stylish life

WHOOP UP YOUR WORKWEAR

Whether dressing for a corporate environment or a more creative industry, it's important to work out your office style. Comfort is crucial and so is fit; say no to shoes that are impossible to walk in, jackets that pinch the armpits and trousers that go up yer bum and other places. Replace with confidence-boosting wardrobe basics that will last the day and feel effortless. Clothes that you can forget about without looking forgettable: like the do-anything dress, the super shirt and the statement skirt (see page 140).

Tailoring can be sleek and stylish, though looser shapes and kimono-styles are perfectly acceptable– and it's always worth investing in an outstanding coat. Grabbing an item off a clothes rail because it's reduced in the sale or will cheer you up (for five minutes) is guaranteed to cost more in the long run. Experience has taught me that the best way to dress well is to dress for your body shape and your lifestyle. These days I prefer considered research to the grab-and-go technique. Updating a favourite silhouette, introducing colour and print and a few knockout accessories is the way to whoop up workwear and still look the business.

Go bold with accessories

'I posted a picture of me wearing a black Comme des Garçons dress with a red purse and people went nuts,' says Lyn Slater, university professor and founder of *accidentalicon.com*, when we discuss clean and simple style. Whether that's good jeans and a blazer or a white shirt and black, wide-leg trousers, this is the ultimate in simple uniform dressing. Yes, the pared-back silhouette is based around the basics, but that doesn't mean blending into the landscape. 'You have to start thinking about make-up and accessories,' continues Slater. 'My palette is neutral, but I will add a really interesting bag, big sunglasses and bold earrings to make an impact.'

Part of minimalist dressing is that it is effortless, comfortable and calm. Accessories may be strong, but they must send out a serious message. Choose embellishments that fit the aesthetic. Slater says: 'You don't want accessories to be the first part of you that people see – so don't overdo it. You want them to blend in, to help make the whole outfit look great.' Think about the bigger picture.

Get creative with colour

If, like me, you prefer the chic-not-shouty approach, then wearing colour can be a bit scary. Much as I admire a strong shade on other women, my palette will usually be minimal to the end. But on the occasions when I do slip a red jumper under my navy blazer or my mustard coat over a navy outfit, I feel a bit of a buzz. Styles and shapes I'm easy with make wearing colour easy. 'I love colour,' states Caroline Issa, chief executive and fashion director at *Tank* magazine and editor-in-chief of *becauselondon.com*. 'Bright fuchsia trousers or a bright pink coat. If I use unexpected colour, I go for a more classic shape.'

Go for the mismatch

As Lisa Salzer says, 'Matchy-matchy is dead,' and the way we live and work today makes it more acceptable to mix genres. Wear a maxi dress and sneakers, slip a blazer on over a jumpsuit, team a sweatshirt with a metallic pleated skirt, or use a leopard print blazer to whoop up a pair of khaki pants. Bring on the bling by donning chandelier earrings and a simple shirtdress or make like Lucinda Chambers and wear socks with kitten heels. A gentle juxtaposition is the quick and easy way to refresh an everyday office wardrobe. It's all about comfort – and the contrast.

Practise with pattern

Often one standout pattern, with the occasional foray into two carefully chosen pieces, is all you need to make the right kind of statement. Try an opulent cocktail coat and a graphic silk scarf, a colourful tweed jacket over a striped dress. Choosing patterns and prints of a similar scale and coordinating one colour from the print with another item of clothing offers a more complementary combination. 'I'm a great believer in matching things up,' declares Lucinda Chambers, fashion director at British *Vogue*, 'I won't do matchy-matchy, but when colours tally up, it looks thoughtful.' But remember, too much detail is just too much. Let's keep it chic, not showy.

Look at brands like: & Other Stories, Missoni, Ganni, Finery, Warehouse Diane von Furstenberg, Marni, Zara, Stella Jean, Sandro, Gestutz.

Practise a new silhouette

Time to start shape-shifting. One attention-grabbing showbiz item is all it takes to give the not-so-basic basics a vital jolt. With the right base layer, the single statement could simply be a shirtdress over wide-leg trousers or a new shirt with bell-shaped sleeves. Try layering a tailored, asymmetric gilet jacket over a long-sleeved T-shirt and cigarette pants, or wear a kimono top with a pencil skirt. Of course, it helps if that eye-catching item is THE right thing, THE trophy piece that's on the money (but which doesn't necessarily cost a fortune) and sprinkles a little modernity onto an office-ready outfit.

Look at brands like: Acne, COS, Roksanda, Ellery, Comme des Garçons, ME+EM, Uterqüe, Sea NY, Paper London, Balenciaga, Reiss, Massimo Dutti.

MICHELLE OGUNDEHIN

'My *ELLE Decoration UK* editor's letter portrait is probably the most high-street ensemble I've ever worn! And I'd generally say I don't do high street. I wore this outfit when I was filming *Grand Designs House of the Year* for British television and I loved the press shot so much, I use it in the magazine every month. The jeans are from Uniqlo, recommended to me for their fit and stretch and, having spent a small fortune on jeans before, they were a revelation. The shirt is from Debenhams, hideously 100 per cent polyester, but I bought a whole set of them in different brights for filming as TV cameras are partial to a bit of colour. They were super-cheap and are resistant to all stains. Being a lover of a gorgeous silk shirt, it's incredibly liberating to be able to spill a drink on your top, wash it under the tap, and have it be pristine and dry again in less than three minutes! The jacket is from Whistles, a very soft, structured number

that fits like a cardi but looks like a jacket. My shoes are Converse All Stars. I really like these – although pre-children I was a dedicated three-inch-plus stiletto-heel wearer. On top I wear a beautiful Max Mara, pale-pink, wool coat. In a year's time, all the above items will no doubt be consigned to the bin, whereas the coat will be a keeper.

The Whistles jacket is re-issued each year in different colours, so I now have a grey and a black one. I don't expect them to last longer than a year though. The blue jacket has already gone – it went all bobbly. The shirt is literally indestructible, and I still wear it as I love the colour, even though I can't bear unnatural fabrics! The jeans, too, are still going strong. I just wish they'd make the same fit and shape in black and grey – I'd buy several pairs of each.

I don't suit shirts that have collars and are buttoned up to the neck or tops with a scooped neckline. Only a collarless V-neck works for me, and yet they're quite hard to find. Diane von Furstenberg used to do one in silk, available in only black and white, but she discontinued them. I had both, but they are aged now and I'm desperate to replace.

I can scrub up exceptionally well for a black-tie do (I have a great photo of me in a sparkly Matthew Williamson dress that I LOVE!), but day-to-day I prefer to be more preoccupied with what I'm doing than what I'm wearing. Clothes that restrict me, require assembly or need to be monitored are not for me. I always wear earrings, but even necklaces start to annoy me by the end of the day (although I have some fabulous ones and adore an embellished neckline). I do rather love a bit of metallic thread running through a dress or top, and gold sandals in the summer.

I am slim and trim by nature as opposed to any effort on my part. I am incredibly lucky, I know. My friends hate me for this.

Editor-in-chief at *Elle Decoration UK*

AMY DE LA HAYE

'

Shirin Guild's skirt square always feels right in different fabrics for different occasions, dressed up or down. I worked with Shirin for ten years. We became friends and she said we had the 'same eyes'. It was this skirt that made me fall in love with her work before I met her. And I have worn it ever since. I really like the simplicity (it is effectively like a poncho taken down to the waist) and it hangs in a style redolent of the period 1916–1919, which I adore. As a dress historian and curator, I am definitely drawn to new clothing that has a historical feel.

The bespoke suit that Emily And (a former tailoring student at the London College of Fashion) made me is so special. The process of commissioning was extraordinary. She asked me for inspiration and without a moment's hesitation I said: 'Yohji Yamamoto meets Redfern (late 19th century British tailor) in the First World War.' The ethos of bespoke has so much integrity – the dreamer in me likes to think, 'If only that could be the future,' but of course it can't. I wear the suit for important lectures and private views. I asked Emily to make me the same skirt in a lighter weight, unlined, navy-blue silk/wool – a year-round fabric that I can also wear more casually.

It was when I was at Brighton University studying dress history that Yohji Yamamoto and Comme des Garçons first showed in Paris and I fell in love with them. I've always found their clothes the most interesting. The fabrics and the shapes are so unusual and sculptural – they are appealing garments to me.

I'm interested in artisan textiles and cross-cultural references. I like clothing from around the world, especially old Indian textiles and vintage silk blouses – or, if they're not vintage, they look like vintage – similar to the ones Sula makes.

Being a curator, I run around a lot, so I need comfortable clothes. I have always bought multiples: Shirin Guild tribal pants, skirt squares and fitted cashmere cardigans with pockets (I like to wear one over the other sometimes, so buy a small and a medium), Sula tops in various colours of the same style. Everything I've bought of Sula's, I live in, I love it. I think her clothes are absolutely beautiful. They're quality without being horrendously expensive. I wear Trippen shoes (multiple slip-on and lace-ups in the same styles) and Ann Demeulemeester leather brogue-style shoes that have a Mary Jane strap and small kitten heel (I don't like that term!) in black and brown.

It's not about spending money; it's about being imaginative. Doing something distinctive. Looking interesting is more important. Knowing what suits you and feeling confident about that. It is entirely personal. To me, it is a slightly historical silhouette – I am definitely drawn to new clothing with a historical feel. It's about having things that are your uniform in a way; they might be unusual garments, but they are your uniform.

Curator, dress historian, author and professor at London College of Fashion

,

CAROLINE ISSA

'I always fall back on the tuxedo. This go-to outfit expresses my love of tailoring and of masculine with a feminine twist. Sometimes I break it down and wear the jacket and trousers separately, but I love a proper 'Helmut Newton' look for the evening, complete with a bow tie, chandelier earrings and a red lip. I have three tuxedos: a white one from Gucci, a black one from Paul Smith and a blue-velvet one from Vacil. I wear the blue-velvet tuxedo jacket with jeans, a T-shirt and clean, white sneakers during the day – or the trousers with a shirt and loafers and chandelier earrings. The Gucci white tuxedo more often comes out at night.

When I'm travelling I tend to wear cashmere track pants (Olivia von Halle has a great tie-waist cashmere tracksuit) – or I layer a silk Equipment shirt with a scarf and wear soft trousers with flat slip-ons. The chandelier earrings come off for the airport scanner!

In my first career as a management consultant, 17 years ago, I dressed very conservatively. I had a brown suit, a black suit, a navy suit and a grey suit. But I always had an understanding of style and the value of design and quality. The first thing I bought when I earned some money was a Jil Sander suit. As I get older I enjoy playing around more; I'm more confident in who I am now and like to express myself more. Style oscillates, but as long as you feel bold and healthy, you can't go wrong.

I love colour. I really enjoy wearing

things like bright fuchsia trousers and a white shirt, or a colourful printed dress and amazing shoes. I love texture – the richer and softer the fabric, the better. One should always invest in great fabrics. Well-crafted and well-made clothes are better for the environment; I believe in value and quality and not throwing my wardrobe out every month.

I tend to use that cliché 'classic with a twist'. It's the style I always go back to. Conservative with a dash! Devices like colour or pattern or a belt or a pair of statement earrings add personality and thoughtfulness. These days I do feel more confident and I like to express myself through my clothes and not follow the old rules.

Chief executive and fashion director at *Tank* magazine

,

LYN SLATER

' A black, well-tailored jacket is one of the core features of my wardrobe. I have a long Yohji Yamamoto black blazer that I could wear every day, forever, and a similar version with cut-out sleeves that I wear with beautifully tailored, black, wide-leg pants. I prefer longer skirts – I have a couple of longer black, A-line skirts. I must have at least 75 white shirts, all different brands, shapes and lengths, all some variation of the classic white shirt. Some are more deconstructed. I totally love one I have from Comme des Garçons and another by Haider Ackermann with long sleeves.

A lot of my clothes are of Japanese design, recycled or vintage pieces from the 1980s and 1990s, and in a black-and-white palette. I wear natural fibres for the most part. I'm conscious of sustain-ability and if designers ask me to wear their stuff, I always look into their manufacturing process first before agreeing.

I have four key style-signifier words: minimalist, monochrome, intellectual, avant-garde. These are the different categories I put objects in and pull from depending on my mood for that day.

The good thing is my signifiers are timeless and I've lived long enough to know that they keep coming back. The white shirt, the black tailored jacket – I know I can get them replaced because they're always going to be in someone's collection.

One of the things I like to do is layer. Layering is where the white shirt comes into play. It's the canvas. Start with one piece and build around that. Everything else is a reaction to that. I'll wear a longer shirt with a wrap-around sweater so that the shirt is more visible – and wide-leg pants or an A-line skirt work very well. I'm really short, so clothing has to go with my body. If you over-layer you can end up looking like you're walking around under a pile of blankets. So I have to be careful – my frame has to support it.

My style is for the real woman who lives in a city – but that doesn't mean you have to look boring. I do like to give off an edge. This is part of my art. I'm still pushing it; I like to take risks, try new things – throw out something people don't expect, but not that far out of range that it's not inclusive.

University professor and founder of *accidentalicon.com*

,

WORKING FROM HOME

Working from home the majority of the week, I want to be comfortable, relaxed and just smart enough to feel focused. The loosening up of modern dress codes suits me right down to a T by Alexander Wang. I've never felt comfortable in formalwear – that's probably why I chose a career in the fashion/media industry where I've never really had to do corporate dressing (or receive a corporate salary). But that's not to say I don't have to look professional and pulled-together when I leave the building.

'You know style when you see it. For me, it's an unspoken thing. It could be a woman walking down the street dressed in jeans and a floppy shirt, but she looks gorgeous. It's how the clothes hang on her body, what shoes she's wearing. You can be elegant and chic when you're wearing a shirt and jeans.'

-

Lyn Slater
University professor and founder of *accidentalicon.com*

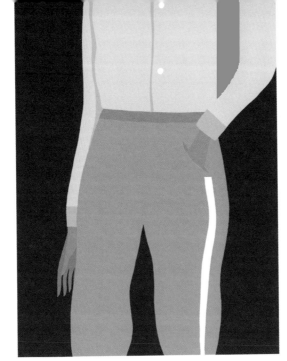

ME+EM, Winser London, Theory, hush, Kit and Ace, James Perse, bassike, Jac + Jack and The Row are perfect for this kind of relaxed, grown-up dressing. Choose sporty separates that are easy and effortless, but smart enough for that all-important business coffee.

How to dress like a gymployee (always fit for work)

Fortunately, the sports-luxe blend of relaxed and formal is the, er, new normal. I may not be as athletic as I once was, but sports-inspired trousers and posh joggers form an integral part of my working wardrobe and trouser suits look top-notch with sneakers. And I like the idea of sportswear sneaking into business class, of going to work in go-faster stripes.

Working from home requires relaxed, easy pieces combined with a smarter element for when you leave the building. Wear luxury track pants with a silk blouse and navy blazer. Try a pull-on-and-go top (see page 146) with harem pants or posh joggers. For an evening event, slip a bomber jacket over a cocktail dress. Mixing and matching (and mismatching) makes an outfit feel modern and less try-hard. Look for quality fabrics with status that can last the day and remain relaxed well into the evening. This is 9-to-9 dressing at its finest. Chic not sloppy is the goal. Clothes that are working not shirking.

Everyday denim

'I'm a denim freak – I've been wearing it since I was five,' says fashion stylist, beauty entrepreneur and model Linda Rodin. 'Never wavered, ever.' And that's the thing: once a denim dame, always a denim dame. Jeans are the mainstay of an everyday outfit and – although occasionally usurped by a fancy new blouse or pair of snazzy shoes – this dependable wardrobe staple always makes the starting line-up. 'Lightweight, heavyweight, one can wear denim all year round,' continues Rodin. 'I build an outfit around jeans. I love all the different styles: bootcut, boyfriend, flared, skinny, I wear them all.'

Doubling up is nothing to the denim lover, adding a matching (or not-quite) shirt, jacket or coat makes perfect sense. Constantly look for new ways to wear this versatile, cotton-twill fabric: from shoes to shirtdresses, culottes to circle skirts, what started out as durable workwear is now accepted as smart-enough, go-to-work wear.

As Rodin points out, 'It's classic, comfortable, packs beautifully and you can just throw it in the washer.' Dependable denim: True Blue, baby... (you know the rest).

Here are six outfit ideas inspired by the wisdom of Linda Rodin:

1. Make it black
Team a black shirt with black, cropped flared jeans (Rodin wears Rachel Comey) and black, low-heeled, round-toe pumps.

2. Wear workwear
Layer dungarees over a denim shirt (Rodin loves Carhartt) and add a bright pair of ballet pumps or brogues to finish.

3. Denim-on-denim
Double up with indigo-blue flared jeans and a matching denim shirt, then elevate the look with red flatform sandals.

4. Vintage style
Team Levi's 501s with turn-ups, skate shoes and an outstanding coat – try faux fur or a brocade/embellished style. For an instant upgrade, swap skate shoes for colourful Mary Janes.

5. Skirting the issue
Wear a knee-length, grey or black denim circle skirt with a neat white shirt tucked in, black opaque tights (pantyhose) and white, heeled ankle boots.

6. Winter wrapped up
Try white skinny jeans (Rodin wears Rag & Bone), an off-white cashmere sweater, pale-gold metallic boots and a big Polar Vortex parka. Sorted, stylish and snug.

'Listen to yourself. Dress according to your lifestyle and the environment you're in.'

-

Pat Cleveland
Model and author

Pyjama dressing

Easy to wear and decadent in a 'Loulou de la Falaise hanging out with Yves Saint Laurent in 1970s Paris' kind of way, pyjama dressing has been wafting around for some time. But to someone who works from home and spends her life in jeans, this kind of casual glamour is hugely appealing.

Silk pyjama-style shirts and patterned kimono jackets add an easy elegance to any outfit. Pair with jeans or matching wide-leg trousers for an excellent everyday ensemble. Alternatively, try slinky, patterned, pyjama-inspired palazzo pants with a roll-neck sweater or cropped round-neck jacket. For evenings, wear pyjama pants with a tuxedo jacket, sparkly earrings and heels to avoid looking like you've just popped out for a pint of milk.

These brands are great places to garner pyjama-rama: Desmond & Dempsey, For Restless Sleepers, Olivia von Halle, hush, Three Graces, Equipment, YOLKE, The Glad Hours.

AMELIA BULLMORE

'When I want to feel good, I reach for my good bits and pieces. It feels like you've got people on your side, somehow, a security net. On a gamine day that's a sweater and jeans. But the sweater needs to be a bit skimpy – I'm small-breasted, the sweater favours the small-breasted – and they've got to be the right jeans. I wear flares, straight leg and skinny styles from Topshop, Levi's and The Kooples. With skinny jeans I'll wear a top that's a bit roomier to get the contrast between top and bottom. I don't wear the same fit twice; so a skimpy top is much better with flared jeans. And I feel much, much better, cooler, chicer, younger in slightly shorter trousers.

Another everyday outfit is a skirt with ankle boots and a T-shirt. Yesterday, I was wearing an old but beautifully fitting pencil skirt, a really nice grey-marl T-shirt with a necklace and these little boots and I felt a million dollars. The boots cost a bomb (they're See by Chloé), but I love them. I look good in A-line skirts and pencil skirts and I look better if the length is on the knee or just above the knee. I have slightly chunky calves, so I don't want anything to hit the calf. I have a selection of posh sweaters (from A.P.C. and Margaret Howell) in cotton or wool. A lot of them are darned, but they are basically the same sweater. If I'm getting dressed in a hurry, I reach for one of these. If there's one thing that crops up again and again, it's this slightly 'mean' sweater. It's good with an A-line skirt, boyish jeans, skinny jeans or mannish-cut trousers. It just works.

Another foolproof outfit is a Vanessa Seward dress for A.P.C., which I got half-price in the sale. I know it's a really good dress, but do I think it's good quality because I know what it's worth? I wear it unbuttoned with the sleeves rolled up and a belt to cinch it in. I've got a waist and, if I'm wearing a dress, I'll show it off.

In winter, I wear Wolford Pure 50 deluxe tights. I say to my husband Paul (the actor Paul Higgins), if you come back as a woman, all you need to know is, 'get those tights'.'

Actor and writer

LINDA RODIN

I'm casual, but I like to feel put-together; I don't like to feel messy or sloppy, but then I don't like to feel uptight either. I always wear jeans. Dark blue denim is my favourite fabric, I never buy pre-washed, and I wear a lot of black – it's a universal look.

I'll wear denim-on-denim. I've been wearing the same denim shirt for 25 years; it has holes in it, but that's the good thing about denim – you can reinforce it when it goes. I bought a wonderful Joseph denim three-quarter-sleeve top in London and I've been wearing it for the last two days with my Levi's 501s. It's charming, like a painter's top, but nipped in at the waist.

I'll go quite funky on the shoes or the coat. I often wear white or silver ankle boots or Adidas sneakers. I love shoes and have loads of pairs, but they have to be comfortable – I don't wear heels any more. I like a Balenciaga-style cocoon coat; I throw it on and instantly feel pulled-together.

My glasses are more necessity than fashion, but I do have fun with them. About eight years ago, I decided to have bifocal, tinted lenses, because I kept losing my other pair. I wear lipstick every day and feel naked without it, like the colour has drained out of my lips. I don't wear face make-up or foundation. I like to keep things quite simple and just have one bold statement. I wear the same jewellery every day: very simple gold rings and necklaces.

I'm always wearing the same clothes – I always look the same. Hair tied back, lipstick, denim. It's a visual thing, I'm not afraid of mixing colour – purple, green, hot pink and silver. But putting an outfit together is like painting; you start with a blank canvas and take it from there.

I'm quite classic; I don't like gimmicks. I don't want to draw attention to myself.

Fashion stylist, beauty entrepreneur and model

GOING OUT

Using a combination of day- and eveningwear to create an outfit with go-anywhere appeal is what I've nicknamed casual glamour. The desired effect is to look modern, chic and a little bit lively – without looking like you've tried too hard. No more changing in the office toilets at the end of a working day. Take one look-at-me, standout piece, like an amazing metallic jacket or a pair of brocade pants, and mix with not-so-basic basics for dressed-up daywear that moves seamlessly into evening. Essential slim-leg black trousers take the edge off a statement jacket, while fancy brocade pants go with a plain silk shirt or cashmere sweater. To me, everyday-wear with a glamorous twist makes complete fashion sense and comes under the mandate of wearing something you always feel right in. Having a fail-safe item of clothing to turn to is more comforting than knowing you've got a lift home and a lie-in. Fact.

The not-too-dressed-up dress

'I went to a big do and my make-up cost more than my dress,' Amelia Bullmore explains. As the British actor and writer is the only famous person I know, I'm quizzing her at her London home about red-carpet events. 'I've never been to the Oscars but I went to the BAFTAs on the bus,' she continues, 'The dress was from Topshop and was pretty inexpensive and the foundation cost me just a few pounds more. It's a long, green, chiffon shirtwaister and I wore it with a ballet-pink belt and COS heels. But I felt really good.'

Feeling comfortable and confident at any event is crucial – whether it's sashaying up the red carpet with the world's paparazzi in tow or as a guest at a wedding with your best friend's dad taking the photos. Keep it chic, simple and modern. The not-so-dressed-up dress provides an instant style switch-up; called upon for work or a particular event to help you look the part and look like yourself. And just because it is a special occasion doesn't mean clothes have to be fussy and frilly. No one wants to look mother-of-the-bride, even when they *are* the mother of the bride (or groom). The aim is to feel relaxed and confident – as if you could go to the BAFTAs on the bus. As Amelia concurs, 'I believe in wearing whatever flatters, whatever you look best in. On another occasion I paid a lot more money for

a Peter Pilotto dress and Chie Mihara shoes, but I felt equally confident both times.' There are many ways to wear a not-so-dressed-up dress. The fuss-free tunic dress and statement necklace is a good, go-anywhere option. The looser A-line or straight-up-and-down shape has the comfort factor and the necklace doesn't have to be a big, flashy diamanté number: try a long pendant necklace or string of beads or pearls. Flat sandals, platforms or flatforms and luxurious lace-ups all look the business.

Ever the tomboy, I was once coerced into wearing a short-sleeved, colour-block shift dress with court shoes. This was for a book promotion shoot for a national newspaper, so hair and make-up was big and bold, too. I've never felt such a frump. A plain shift with a bit of stretch and a lovely bracelet sleeve would've been so much more chic. Choose something in navy blue, emerald green, burnt orange or a gorgeous shade of pinky-red. Think Roksanda on a budget and head straight to COS. Go for heeled shoes in a colour or pattern that mismatches the dress ever so slightly: adding contrast will dial down the look.

Or take the BAFTAs-on-the-bus approach and wear a long dress with a belt and fancy flats. Loosen things up by unbuttoning the skirt of a shirtdress and wearing over flared trousers.

The timeless tuxedo

It's always been my dream to own a tuxedo to look as slick as a Parisian woman wearing Yves Saint Laurent. To make like Anjelica Huston in the 1970s (*The Jack Years*) in a super-cool burgundy trouser suit and matching silk blouse. The dream was partly realised when I splurged on my once-in-a-lifetime Céline tuxedo jacket that I love to wear with jeans (see page 144), but for a super-sharp evening ensemble, it's grand to go head-to-toe. From Saint Laurent's 1970s muse, Betty Catroux, to Tilda Swinton today, this feminine take on masculine tailoring reveals the unerring power of the pantsuit. This is a conversation I continue with a tuxedo-wearing, fashion-editor friend from my Hearst magazine days: 'The classic silhouette of the black tuxedo is both sexy and powerful,' says Claudette Prosper. 'I feel extremely self-assured in this aesthetic. It's a style staple for me that I can construct for the cocktail hour or deconstruct for a day at the office, simply by wearing flats or high-rise stilettos, or slipping a pussy-bow or a camisole underneath.'

Take your pick of tuxedos at: Gabriela Hearst, Pallas, Yves Saint Laurent, ME+EM, Jigsaw, Vacil, Paul Smith.

The get-up-and-go jumpsuit

For work, weekend, whatever, the jumpsuit is an oh-so easy option – in fact, I'm sitting in a chambray version and clogs as I write this. With three more boilersuits in the wardrobe, and counting, I'm turning into a bit of an all-in-one obsessive. Add a pair of chandelier earrings and upgrade the footwear to transform this working-from-home wardrobe into an effortless evening look. For me, time saved getting dressed outweighs the toilet trauma. When in doubt, get a jumpsuit out. Just allow plenty of time when you go to the bathroom.

Jumpsuit joy: hush, Bliss and Mischief, Zara, M.i.h Jeans, Stella McCartney, Citizens of Humanity, Winser London.

Shoes that go with jumpsuits

Be warned: not every shoe looks good with a jumpsuit. Fancy flats, sneakers, hi-tops, flatform sandals and heeled ankle boots are the way to go. I particularly love Penelope Chilvers' Cubana boot (a velvet ankle boot with a Cuban heel). 'Roll the trouser leg up – you need to see the top of the boot,' advises Chilvers. See also Chapter 4, Flat shoes forever (see page 88).

The right going-out shoes

Wearing stylish, run-around shoes gives an outfit go-anywhere appeal (go-anywhere without having to nip into the nearest pharmacy for a packet of Band-Aids) and it works for me. From conference call to cocktail party, comfort dressing with a casually glamorous twist is the way to go. Fortunately there are tons of gorgeous shoes that are *au courant*, chic and easy to walk or stand around at a party in. Make the most of cocktail sneakers, decorative flats, velvet slippers, Moroccan babouche slippers, flatforms, kitten, block or mid heels. Remember, no one looks glamorous when their feet hurt. See Chapter 4, Flat shoes forever (see page 88).

Where to find them: Repetto, Rogue Matilda, Tabitha Simmons, Georgina Goodman, ViBi Venezia, Pretty Ballerinas, Le Monde Beryl, Gucci, Roger Vivier, By Far, Aquazzura, Tod's, Boden, Nicholas Kirkwood, Ellery, Rachel Comey.

PAT CLEVELAND

'I like to go out to an evening event and get dressed up. I want to have my eyelashes on, my heels and an evening dress, because I think it's important to have that kind of time; that night-time with people, that's so different from the work day. I like to feel like a woman, to have moments where I express my femininity.

One of my favourite things is a Stephen Burrows dress from the collection he did with 'lettuce hems'. It's a really colourful rainbow-striped jersey, very playful and very me. If I have to go to an event, I'll wear something vintage; it's not like I have to carry the labels of today – I will if I'm modelling, because that's my work – but I don't go out of my way for advertising.

My clothes are important to me because they get me out of the house! When I look at my wardrobe, items remind me of different times in my life. I remember those moments so passionately. I've given a lot of my clothes to museums; the ones I've kept are not always the best pieces, but they mean something to me. The people who made the clothes, the designers, made them for me. Having these clothes is like one step beyond a dream – it gives you a chance to be something.

I take care of clothes, even when they're older – that's how I am. I sew things back together.

Most of my Halston was stolen – so girls, don't let people house-sit when you're away because you might find your clothes get sold to a second-hand store on Second Avenue and end up on a drag queen in Germany (which is what happened to me!).

I love costume jewellery – although I've had diamonds given to me and wearing them is a beautiful thing, it's not a necessity for me in my life now.'

Model and author

CLAUDETTE PROSPER

My personal style straddles the masculine/feminine aesthetic. I love the mannish trouser suit turned on its head by imposing feminine pieces, like a blouse or camisole and heels. Even if I wear a dress or a skirt, I pair it with a tailored tuxedo jacket. I love to wear drop earrings and I always wear make-up. I feel this is a must because I shave my hair and I think this accentuates my facial features. Simple highlights of eyes, lips and brows complete my look.

I'm a savvy shopper, so when I find a bargain, I buy it in duplicate. I have several pussy-bow blouses, crisp white shirts, camisoles, brogues and black trousers – and more than 10 tux-style jackets. My philosophy for this is two-fold: firstly, because of my love for a piece and the knowledge that I'll wear it multiple times; and, secondly, because of my size. For example, shoes! It's a nightmare finding shoes big enough for my size 42s, so when I do, I'll buy two pairs.

I would describe my figure as large, shapely and in proportion. I am tall-ish – 5 ft 8 in (1.73 m) – with long limbs and a small waist. I mostly wear a straight or wide-legged trouser or an A-line or full-skirted dress as I feel these silhouettes flatter my shape best.

Fashion journalist and stylist

ANNA GARNER

I love dresses. I love the simplicity of wearing a dress and the silhouette a dress gives. I have a Mother of Pearl dress that I wear a lot. It's quite formal – midi length in a tiny floral print, stretch-cotton fabric with a high collar – but I'll wear it dressed down with boots or sneakers and an old Marni cardigan over the top. It's quite a high-waisted style, but it's timeless: long-sleeved, very fitted and always feels put-together. If I don't really know what to wear, that's very much a go-to piece. For a special occasion I wear it with chunky stack heels, probably Marni, and one big cuff or bold earrings.

I do think the idea of balance is really important. The dress also needs a bit of contrasting so it doesn't look too prim – it's that attitude thing – I have a little cropped, vintage denim jacket that I might sling over the top. The colour palette is an interesting combination of pale blues, black, burgundy and brown, so it picks out all the seasons and works year-round. I'm not normally one for wearing florals or prints – I love monochrome – but this works because of the silhouette of the dress. It's a bit, 'Job done!'

I'm quite a plain dresser in many ways, I love a cropped pair of trousers to wear with sneakers or boots or heels. I tend to go for simpler silhouettes with unexpected shoes. I have a pair of burgundy Marni boots with a pink heel that I love. I'm not into flouncy or flimsy dresses, but if you get the right one, you can feel very chic and elegant.

Style needs to be a very natural thing, an extension of your personality. It's a spontaneous affair – what you feel at that moment, how you want to express yourself that day. My style has stayed quite similar for most of my adult life: pared down with a quirk. I'm happy with my figure: English with a bit of pear thrown in.

Former fashion director at Selfridges, Joseph and Henri Bendel's and founder of *thegarnered.com*

Flat shoes forever

FANCY FLATS

I take a zero-tolerance approach to sore feet. As a comfy-shoe obsessive, with the Pinterest board to prove it, I'm always on the lookout for easy, run-around styles. I'm 53 and would rather wear Liberty print Nike Air Max than nan shoes. To paraphrase George Bernard Shaw: 'If a woman rebels against high-heeled shoes, she should take care to do so in a pair of fancy flats.'

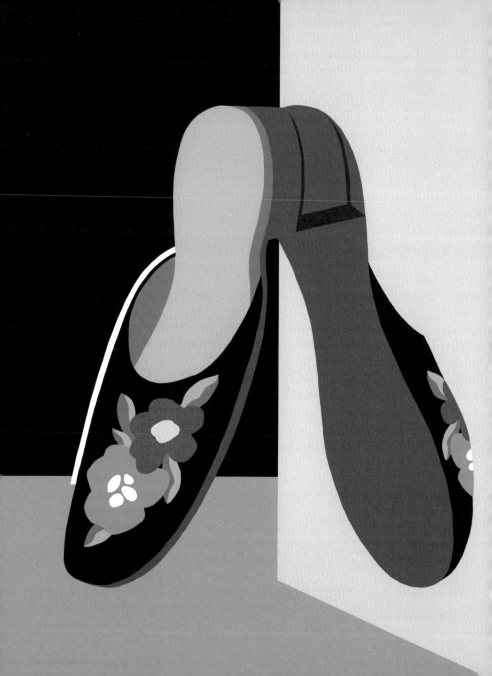

Comfy shoes don't mean you have to sacrifice style, particularly now there's a powerful demographic of women who want to look good in shoes they can walk in. Personally, I think fabulous flats are here to stay, but just to make sure I asked Hannah Rochell, author of *En Brogue: Love Fashion, Love Shoes, Hate Heels* for her opinion: 'Sooner or later designers will want the exact opposite of what everyone is wearing, so no doubt heels will come back. But I don't think the woman on the street will necessarily feel like she has to wear them. The last few seasons have been a liberating time for those of us who would rather wear flats – particularly as brands are putting so much more effort into designing them. So yes, I think the demand for flat shoes will stay put.'

Hannah Rochell's five favourite flat shoe brands:

Grenson – I love this brand for smart shoes with a twist. The styles with a white Vibram sole are really practical and look cool. I've worn mine in the rain and snow and they're still going strong.

Rose Rankin – if you want to dabble with trainers but aren't up for a full sporty look, these are brilliant. The white Cony sneakers go with everything: they're leather, subtle in design and beautifully made.

Clarks Originals – stick to the Originals range for classic, cool styles. Desert boots are always a winner, or for something more modern, I adore the Trigenic Flex trainers. They are incredibly comfortable and strangers will stop you in the street and ask you where you got them.

Northern Cobbler – great shoes with an attention to detail that's second-to-none. I've worn Northern Cobbler brogues to weddings as an alternative to more feminine flats. They also make stunning sandals and trainers.

Tabitha Simmons – I'm listing this brand as an inspiration more than anything else. These are the most beautiful pointed flats but they are expensive. Do some research to find similar on a smaller budget (try French Sole and Office). Otherwise, save up and check the sales!

How to wear flat shoes

Footwear designer Penelope Chilvers counts Alexa Chung, Rihanna and Cate Blanchett as fans. Her own personal approach to style begins at the bottom, 'I always start with the shoes. I love mixing vintage with new and like to have a vintage piece in every outfit. My everyday uniform for designing in my studio is jeans and a men's shirt with a row of boots by the door for walking the dog, running for the bus, getting out or into the country.' Here, the designer of fabulous, run-around shoes offers eight tips on how to wear flats:

1. A long, flowing 1920s-style silk pyjama trouser and a velvet slipper can look super-glam in the evening.

2. I love the androgynous look that a wide trouser can give. Trousers with turn-ups and mannish styles look great with Chelsea boots or brogues.

3. Culottes look fab worn with long, equestrian-style boots.

4. Wear velvet shoes in summer.

5. Look for boots that are cut low on the ankle; these look good with a skirt.

6. Wear a slipper-style with an A-line leather skirt or a pleated midi and a sweatshirt or silk T-shirt.

7. Flats usually look best with a break and some flesh or a sock showing between the shoe and the trouser hem. Wear cigarette pants or roll the legs of your trousers up.

8. Wear fancy socks with loafers; colourful pop socks or fishnet styles with slippers.

Where to find fabulous flat shoes: Church's, Grenson, Malone Souliers, Clarks, O'Keeffe, ATP Atelier, Coclico, Gucci, J.M. Weston, Tod's, FEITN, Camper, Senso, Jaggar Footwear.

The flatform phenomenon

'The flatform has elevated the idea of a flat shoe in women's minds,' explains Alison Hargreaves, head of marketing for Grenson, as we walk briskly across town. She's wearing a pair of black leather, 1940s-inspired flatform sandals and a khaki summer dress and looks incredibly chic. 'I've got a bit of height and it's comfortable and it's a nice shoe. What's not to like?'

The low wedge or flatform has been one of the breakthrough styles of the decade (as well as one of Grenson's bestsellers), elegantly bridging the gap between flat, structured shoes and sneakers. 'I wear them with cropped jeans, wide trousers and dresses and don't have to think about it too much,' continues Hargreaves. 'If I go away, I always pack a pair; they're a good way to dress things up without taking it too far.' Versatility, comfort and ease are three comfy shoe considerations. 'There's less deliberation,' Hargreaves goes on. 'I don't have to think, "Does it look chic? How long will I be standing up? Where's the contrast?" It's the perfect mix – a smart shoe that feels like a sneaker.'

'Mixing proportion and silhouette is fun – anything goes. I have a beautiful long, flowy Céline skirt that I wear with a neat white shirt and flatforms. It only looks good with a clumpy shoe; the balance isn't quite right with ballet flats.'

-

Linda Rodin
Fashion stylist, beauty entrepreneur and model

Make the most of mid-heels

'The days of running around in uncomfortable shoes are over,' declares footwear designer Tracey Neuls when we meet in her shop in London's Marylebone. 'I think it's ridiculous. It impairs women and I don't think there's anything sexy about being in pain at work or while you're walking around.' When we have stuff to do and places to go, we need footwear that works, and Neuls is well known for creating wearable shoes with wow factor. Here's her advice:

Don't go for more than a 55 mm (2 in) height heel: I don't design shoes higher than that and think that after that point you can't build any comfort into it – other than a taxi or a chair. It's just not a functioning shoe. It's good if the heel is a little bit more substantial at the place where you hit the ground. You don't teeter so much.

Shoes can be like jewellery: You don't need to match them to an outfit – they can stand on their own and work as a contrast. I think it's fab if you get flashy shoes that don't match, like our neon-red lace-up. You wouldn't think 'I'm not going to wear my ruby ring today, I haven't got anything to go with it.' Wear shoes with confidence. Don't wonder if they go – they do.

Get the fit right: The only time you're not in shoes is when you're in bed (hopefully). Like underwear, shoes are so close to your body – the foundation of everything you do in the day – so they have to fit correctly. Once you find a shoe that's comfortable, the addiction level is unstoppable. In order to find a good fit, get yourself to a specialist, whether that's a specialist in eyewear, a specialist in make-up or a specialist in footwear. There's a lot that goes into shoemaking and a reason it's still a craft.

Look for something with versatility: Find shoes that you can wear with ankle socks and a skirt, three-quarter-length leggings or rolled-up jeans. As long as you feel that you've added a bit of personality, there's no formula. I don't think a sexy shoe is always a stereotypical thing; you can get a lot of personality, individuality and beauty into an object that doesn't need to be painstaking as well. It's better to show a bit of ankle than to have straight-leg trousers coming right down and meeting the shoes – that just makes the whole outfit look dumpy.

Wearable shoes: things to look out for

Whether you're going for flats, low wedges or mid-heel shoes, there are certain things worth considering before you hand over the cash.

You get what you pay for

Buy flimsy footwear with no support and soles as thin as a politician's promise and expect to crank up the Uber account. Choose quality leather uppers and sturdy soles and be sure to go above and beyond the 10, 000 steps per day mark. It's always worth thinking about the stuff that's on the inside, too, like cushioned insoles or having a metal shank. Some cheap shoes use plastic or eliminate the shank altogether, reducing the support offered. Look for shoes with a leather lining – specifically cow leather, as pig leather tends to sweat more and is naturally smelly (who knew?). 'A well-made pair can get better with time,' points out footwear designer Penelope Chilvers. 'If they are well looked after, shoes will keep their shape, take on character and become so familiar they'll be like old friends.'

Invest in ageless styles

Buy velvet slippers, Chelsea boots, brogues, mid-heel ankle boots in eye-catching fabrics. 'We call it "utilitarian glamour"', says designer Tracey Wells. 'And it's not too overtly bling, just quietly seductive.' Again, she emphasises longevity. 'Choose something individual, something beautiful, that will last,' adds Neuls. 'Customers want to grow old with their shoes, not bored with them.'

Heel height matters

If the pitch is wrong, it will throw you off balance. Avoid styles with a steep incline.

Avoid the faff factor: The older I get, the less inclined I am to engage in a shoe switch-up (wearing run-around shoes and carrying a fancy pair of heels in a bag). Avoid strappy styles and extreme bunion-provoking points and remain footloose and faff-free!

'I always get drawn to
the same colour
palettes: monochrome
with a flash of colour.
I like bold colours:
red, olive green and
metallic gold.
I've got some beautiful
burgundy, Marni boots
with a pink heel
that I wear with a pair of
camel cropped trousers.'

Anna Garner
Founder of thegarnered.com

Sneaking into style

In the 1970s, wearing sneakers was a subversive act. Now sportswear has gone mainstream and pimped-up sneakers are a mainstay of many designer collections. Women are now buying more sneakers than high heels, and that's a fact. The sports shoe has gone from casual outsider to modern staple. Soothing news to anyone who rates being able to walk the distance over taxi shoes. Here's how to get your kicks and score some serious style points.

Style it out in skate shoes: Go for the Grace Coddington approach and wear statement slip-ons with an all-black outfit. Cropped, ankle-flashing trousers (or a jumpsuit with rolled-up legs) work best. In winter, choose draught-proof cigarette pants or leggings to prevent a north-westerly up the nether regions. And skate shoes can be worn with tunic dresses. Just look for slim leather styles that aren't as wide as a skateboard and wear with opaque tights and an outstanding coat.

Six of the best skate shoes: Vans, Superga, Pierre Hardy, Céline, Common Projects, Clarks.

Classic sneakers never go out of style: Juxtaposing Stan Smiths with sharp tailoring gives officewear a modern edge. Team a deconstructed trouser suit with a T-shirt to help avoid the Tess McGill (played by Melanie Griffith in *Working Girl*) vibe. For the perfect preppy look, try plimsolls with a pair of bright khaki pants and a shirt. Trousers that are bootcut, have a slightly flared leg shape or are a slouchy gentlewoman-style look fantastic with sneakers.

Hi-top heaven: Choose baseball boots with a more elegant, streamlined shape that won't make it look like you've wrapped your feet in the duvet. Go for seventies Patti Smith-style with Converse Chuck Taylors, black skinny jeans and a biker jacket, or subvert a floral-print maxi dress with a grey-marl hooded top and classic cream hi-tops. Give hi-tops an uptown spin with culottes or cropped trousers and a blazer.

Opt for old-school: Adidas Stan Smiths and Gazelles, Nike Cortez, Puma States, Superga Cotu Classic, Converse All Stars, New Balance 420, Common Projects, Zespa, Eytys.

Half a dozen hi-tops: Converse All Stars, Common Projects, Rose Rankin, Pierre Hardy, Nike Blazer, Golden Goose Deluxe.

Accessories: bring on the bling

BRING ON THE BLING

The opening soundtrack of the late Albert Maysles' documentary *IRIS* is the wonderful jangle of the nonagenarian New Yorker's jewellery. Iris Apfel is getting dressed. Putting the max into maximalism. Piling on the big, bold, beaded necklaces as multiple bangles on both wrists rattle. There's choreography, though, to this pick-and-mix approach, a sense of coordination. Apfel may be loud and proud, but she's an attentive curator.

'If you're going to wear bold jewellery, then you have to select wisely,' says Anna Garner, former fashion director at Selfridges, Joseph and Bendels and founder of luxury website *thegarnered.com*. 'Mixing colours and jewels can work really well, but proceed with caution: you have to feel confident and it needs to suit your personality. Focus on one or two amazing pieces – like a big cuff or beautiful necklace – and let them stand out.'

From Iris Apfel's well-curated baubles to Garner's simple gold rings and necklaces, we all have a signature style. What matters most is that it's personal to you and is something you love. Jewellery doesn't have to cost a fortune; most of mine is cheap, cheerful and of the costume variety. I have a few silver bits and pieces – bracelets, hoop earrings and one long, handmade, silver pendant necklace – and the most beautiful Junghans men's watch with a dark-blue leather strap. But it's a pair of old diamanté, dangly earrings that get the most compliments. The posts are bent and the backs are tarnished, but the sparkly, uplifting effect is still the same. These statement earrings are so old that I can't remember where they're from, but I do know they're high street, very 'me' and the perfect way to temper a blazer or mannish shirt.

For most women, a little goes a long way and the pile-it-on approach can be a bit too flamboyant. But chutzpah can be introduced into the most minimal of wardrobes. The aim to look cool and pared-down, not like you've been accessorised by a six-year-old.'

Women who wear it well

Loulou de la Falaise

The late Loulou de la Falaise instinctively knew what went with what and realised the power of a statement necklace. And earrings. And a cuff bracelet. This maximalist approach, with all its baubles and beads, makes simple outfits look extraordinary.

Nancy Cunard

Renowned for her decorative bangles, and other antics, Nancy Cunard used an armful of accessories to make a political statement. Fine for a lady of leisure at the turn of the 20th century, not so handy if working on a laptop today. However, for parties and social occasions, this is a perennially stylish look.

Gloria Steinem

Though I'm sure Steinem doesn't want to be defined by what she's wearing, admiring her enduring image – as well as her eloquence and humour – doesn't detract from a brilliant career. The cream silk shirt, Aviator glasses, pendant necklace, jeans, and perfect blow dry all add up to impeccable, age-defying style.

Six of the best places to find costume jewellery: Nocturne, Diana Broussard, J.Crew, Toolally Jewellery, Annie Costello Brown, Mango.

Six purveyors of precious jewellery: Astley Clarke, Laura Lee, Delfina Delettrez, Anna Quan, Aurélie Bidermann, Jessica McCormack.

'I love Pippa Small jewellery.
I always admire women
with beautiful jewellery
and good grooming.
Having well-groomed hair is
important; it makes you
feel ready to go. A well-ironed
shirt and good hair can
make you feel decently dressed.
I love print and have a huge
collection of silk scarves.
The short scarf has come back.
And I'm ready! I love
men's silk evening scarves in
paisley prints or polka dots, too.'

-

Penelope Chilvers
Footwear design

How to layer jewellery

Wearing two necklaces, four rings, two bracelets and three earrings, Lisa Salzer likes her jewellery layered up. 'I believe in wearing multiple pieces,' says the designer and founder of Lulu Frost jewellery, 'not arbitrarily piling on volume, but wearing pieces that have meaning. Jewellery that tells a story and you might have fun telling.' Frost is wearing an 18-carat rose-gold Lulu Frost bracelet (a gift-to-self and celebration of 10 years in business) with a vintage Bakelite bracelet, Moroccan antique earrings bought on her honeymoon and an antique stud from her grandma. The simple

navy outfit and black clogs provide the perfect backdrop to Lisa's layering; the overall effect is interesting and modern and doesn't look too much. 'I love the idea of a neutral wardrobe: blacks, whites and navy, staying away from too much colour. I prefer to have interesting textures and sculptural cuts so the jewellery speaks for itself.'

In order to achieve this cool, but not cluttered, look, Salzer shares her advice. 'Don't follow trends – have a jewellery identity and layer in the trend with your classic look. I wouldn't want to follow a trend completely

but I'd mix it in with my individual pieces. It's about authenticity, wearing what you've always worn and being comfortable with that.'

Salzer suggests shopping high–low and mixing high street with designer. 'Don't go with all one designer or a carbon copy of an ad campaign. Mix something fancy with something simple.' You can also mix materials, metals and textures. 'There are no rules, but sticking to one tone is very old-school, which is fine if you're going to a costume party as Nancy Reagan but, generally speaking, the rules from the past don't apply any more.'

Salzer thinks 'hands tell a story'. Clothing doesn't cover them, so they're visible and they're a place to wear delicate jewellery. She suggests using asymmetry to keep things interesting: 'Stack rings so each finger is different: two on one finger, three on the other. I like unexpectedness.'

Finally, 'wear a bold necklace with a bold outfit – I love the idea of accentuating a strong piece, but it has to be tempered; there's only so much boldness one can take. Keep hair and make-up simple. Three bold pieces is probably enough to make an outfit unforgettable.'

SARAH-JANE ADAMS

'I very rarely wear jewellery as, having been an antique jewellery dealer all my adult life, I sense the symbology and deep meaning and am not able to carry the weight of the messages imbibed. I don't wear plastic, base metals, fake gemstones or rhinestones. Perhaps some would say I'm a jewellery snob but, for me, it is more a matter of curation and representation.

For as long as I can remember, I have chosen to wear pre-worn, mended garments. My favourite piece is a tattered, threadbare, 1920s, satin jacket; I believe it was modified in the 1940s. The reason I keep and wear the clothes I do is because memories held in a long-worn garment touch my psyche, whereas mass-produced uniforms leave me cold. Clothes are, after jewellery, the major way I store memories.

All my clothes get a good amount of wear. Repairing rather than replacing is my way. I have some pieces with patches on the patches, darning on the darning. I have multiples of items such as Indian embroidered skirts, kimonos, Adidas jackets, cotton T-shirts. I spend very little on clothes, a little more on shoes. I love Adidas Originals sneakers and enjoy mixing their collaborative pieces (Jeremy Scott, Rita Ora, Mary Katrantzou) with my eclectic wardrobe.

I have always dressed differently. Clothing has been my friend, my protector, my weapon, my armour. What I wear has helped me lead a fulfilling life, moving with ease across cultures whilst reflecting my passion as a human being.

Antique jewellery dealer, traveller and Instagram star '

LITTLE TOUCHES
LIVEN THINGS UP

The joy of scarves

Scarves are instant game-changers, a quick and easy way to add flair. 'Colour is almost more important than the design,' maintains scarf designer Jane Carr. 'We take care to make prints and colours flattering next to the face. The balance of colours and the harmony is hugely important to us.' Like jewellery, what you're wrapping round your neck and wearing next to your face needs to suit both complexion and character.

'What's brilliant these days is that you can be inspired in so many ways – a scarf tied on a bag or around a wrist, worn prim Parisian-style or more nonchalant with a leather jacket.'

The skinny scarf:

Feeling slightly underdressed on my way to a fashion show recently, I perked up a normcore jacket and jeans with a slim pink-paisley silk scarf from Paul Smith. Long and lean is a timeless, year-round option – think cool-as-you-like Anita Pallenberg and Keith Richards, sharing scarves in the 1970s (I do when I wear Mr That's Not My Age's accessories). This style goes with everything: trouser suits, tuxedo jackets, jumpsuits, dresses, silk blouses, T-shirts. And there are many ways to get the skinny – wrap around the neck once with the two ends hanging down, or loop one end through the other in a very loose knot. Wear a nonchalantly tied side knot, or let it hang loose: like it's there, and you just don't care...

The headscarf

Perfect for bad hair days and a quick post-beach makeover. A cotton scarf has more traction than silk and can be simply folded, as per the neckerchief. Either tie in a jaunty knot at the top of the head for a retro 1950s vibe or knot at the nape of the neck for more of a 'Bardot in St Tropez' headband. Clashing prints and colourful styles always look fabulous, and a pair of statement earrings feels very Stella Jean.

The foulard

A bit John Wayne, a bit French *femme*; take a large silk square, fold in half and knot at the back, allowing the scarf to drape loosely at the front. Go for Parisian over Western styling by twisting rather than knotting at the back, and bringing both ends forward (one on either side of the neck). This works particularly well if you're wearing a blazer or V-neck T-shirt, or work in an office with the air-conditioning cranked up. It is definitely the best way to prevent draughts around the décolletage.

Where to find the best neckwear: Missoni, Lily and Lionel, Liberty, Zara, hush, Rohka, Hermès, agnès b, Jane Carr, Auntie Oti, Denis Colomb, Jo Gordon.

The wrap-around

Upgrade any travel wardrobe with a large, patterned, cotton or lightweight-wool scarf. Whoosh loosely around the neck, over a plain T-shirt and khaki military jacket, at the airport. And for in-flight mode, ignore the complimentary travel blanket and simply loosen the scarf, draping it over the shoulders like a shawl. This multi-tasking summer style also comes in handy as a sarong at the beach and can be thrown over a neck and shoulders that have seen too much sun. Add one to your holiday checklist, now.

The neckerchief

My preferred way to wear a scarf right now is neckerchief-style. The last time I embraced this jaunty look was as a teenage Debbie Harry fan with a bandanna and a second-hand biker jacket. Since then, my vintage leather has been upgraded to Isabel Marant, and for a modern update on the neckerchief I've been looking at Margaret Howell's two-colour spot silk scarf. Try a neckerchief with a super shirt and capri pants; add a pair of chunky sandals to bring the look bang up-to-date. Just fold the scarf in half and keep folding until you have a neat band, tie in a knot at the side of the neck – or at the front – and leave the two longer ends. Wrap around and knot at the front to neaten things up.

A bit on bags

I've never really been interested in fancy, look-at-me designer handbags. Paying silly money for leather accessories to dangle from an elbow is just not my thing. But, as designer Ally Capellino observes, 'A bag is part of your outfit, part of what you're wearing.' It can also be a reflection of who you are. As a fan of faff-free style, the cross-body bag is chic, reliable and the perfect companion for running around with. Hands-free, that's me.

On workdays, I often carry a small leather cross-body bag and a leather tote. 'Everyone in Japan does that two bag thing,' continues Capellino. 'If I'm travelling, I'll have a little bag for my phone, passport and money. I like to wear the strap quite short, like a drug dealer – you can tell where I live! But backpacks are just as valid.

You can put stuff in without them breaking your shoulder. A businesswoman definitely needs a posh backpack, particularly if she's going to change shoes.' Choose a colour that goes with everything, Capellino recommends: dark green, dark chocolate brown (which the Italians call *testa di moro*) and white. To this I would add navy, grey, and for a small leather cross-body bag, red.

Where to find the best 'chic not shouty' bags: Agnes Baddoo, Mimi Berry, Mansur Gavriel, Milli Millu, A.P.C., Coach, J&M Davidson, M.Hulot, Village England, Jigsaw, London Edit, Valextra.

Belt up

Belts have a purpose: to hold trousers up, keep a voluminous dress or shirt in check and add a colourful contrast to any outfit. They also come in handy on holiday, if your suitcase breaks. Often a quick, easy and reasonably priced way to dial things up a notch, belts add polish but are not about neatness. The aim is to perk up an outfit rather than deaden it with a business-like band.

'Always have a belt! I love accessories and wouldn't wear trousers with belt loops without one,' says Lucinda Chambers, fasion director at British *Vogue.*

Here are three popular belt styles and some fantastic ways to wear them:

The plain leather belt

Lee Miller wore hers through the loops of wide tapered trousers with a silk tunic shirt tucked in; Kate Moss with rose-pink satin capri pants, a black shirt and black patent-leather heeled pumps. Do not be fooled by the simplicity of this style – the plain leather belt is one of the stealthiest fashion accessories out there. I have an A.P.C. one in black leather, 3 cm (1¼ in) wide, with a simple silver metal buckle; it's at least 20 years old and is never going to wear out. This is a belt for life that will add polish to an everyday look.

Is there a better combination than the tan leather belt and double denim? I don't think so. They are two not-so-basic basics that go together beautifully. Just add stone suede ankle boots and you're good to go. Try a wide belt around the waist of a maxi skirt with a long-sleeved T-shirt loosely tucked in (this also works with a sash belt) and Converse All Stars or flat sandals. Or with a patterned pencil skirt, denim shirt and mid-heels. Match the belt colour to one of the background colours of the pencil-skirt print. Belts look great through the belt loops of a pair of combat pants; add a stripy T-shirt and strappy sandals, Lucinda Chambers-style.

The wrap-around

There is something eminently rakish and charming about this long, slim leather style. I'm picturing Barbara Hepworth grafting on a sculpture in men's workwear and a spotty headscarf with a belt knotted around her waist. Or Inès de la Fressange outside Paris Fashion Week in a navy blazer, T-shirt, Roger Vivier buckled flats and a red leather belt buckled and twisted through the loops of her chinos. This slim leather style is long enough to wrap around, buckle up and tuck casually under so that the end hangs down. Wear one around a single-breasted coat, tailored gilet or jacket (another very Inès thing to do), cinch in a tunic dress or add as a focal point on pleated or paper-bag waist trousers.

Keep it loose and carefree and not too constricted. The wrap-around belt should tie an outfit together, but not too tightly.

Obi, sash and ribbon belts

Admittedly, I haven't worn one of these since the 1980s – when my dad's cummerbund made the perfect addition to a New Romantic get-up – but with all the pyjama dressing and loose layering that's around, it's only a matter of time. Traditional Japanese fabric styles have a colourful contrast on the reverse, accentuate the waist and hold a kimono together (and this also works with an edge-to-edge jacket).

The obi/sash belt also comes in soft leather and doesn't have to be reserved for eastern-inspired outfits. In the 1950s, American designer Claire McCardell used belts over her simple, sporty dresses and playsuits; by the 1980s they decorated Yves Saint Laurent's satin evening gowns and Claude Montana's long, luxurious coats. Try a military jacket with a metallic belt, a plain black band over a striped shirtdress, or add a karate-inspired black belt to an ivory Armani trouser suit à la Cate Blanchett. Alternatively, keep it neat by colour-matching a wide belt to a tailored jacket. Think *Nightclubbing*-era Grace Jones. Then kick some ass.

Where to find the best belts: J&M Davidson, Shinola, Gucci, Moschino, Mulberry, Maje, A.P.C., Prada, Doe Leather, Hope.

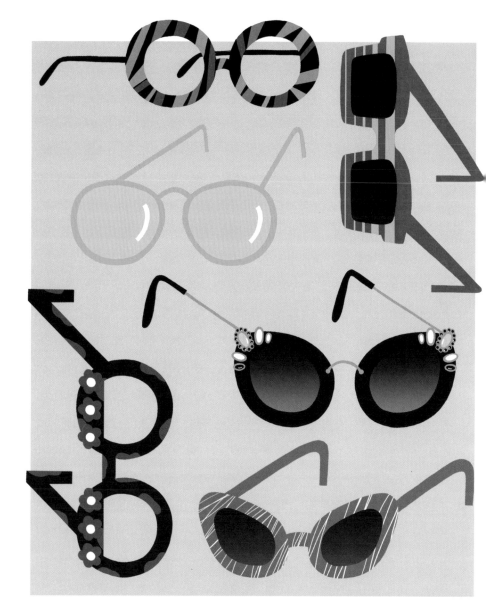

CHOOSING THE
RIGHT GLASSES

When we meet, Marie Wilkinson, design director at Cutler and Gross, is wearing a beautiful pair of 1950s-style brick-red frames. 'They're called A Day at the Races,' she tells me, 'I was thinking about jockeys and how they want to be distinctive but don't wear logos, just vivid colours. The colours are very dense, very high pigment, so you can see them from far away.' Having worked with the eyewear brand for 33 years, and worn glasses since the age of eight (when her mother noticed she was sitting very close to the television), Marie has experimented with a range of different styles: from pink 1960s 'kitten eye' to round acetate frames in glittery black. Eulogising over eyewear as a glamorous fashion accessory rather than a mere 'medical appliance', she offers advice on what to look for when buying new frames.

Fit, size and shape

First, the basics: 'Ensure the glasses frame the eyes and the eyes are the focus and sit centrally in the eye rim.' Then you can start thinking about shape. 'If you want something to open up your face, choose frames with a wider shape. For a small face, I would suggest an oversized, fine-rimmed metal frame for a playful take on proportion, or an immaculately fitting acetate frame.

If you go for something bold then make sure it follows a natural line on the face – it could be a fringe, your eyebrows, jawline or cheekbones. There is something to celebrate on everyone's face. The classic kitten eye is a recurring theme for me; it works with my hairstyle. If it's the eyebrows, then ensure the frame follows the brow line, and runs just underneath the brow line to emphasise its sweep.'

Complement your look

Glasses are part of your complete look, so consider how they work with your make-up and clothes. 'Choose a colour that makes the eyes pop and enhances the iris colour. Like make-up, eyewear is a positive way to add colour to your face. If your signature lipstick is non-negotiable, then work with the lipstick. Make sure the frames are an opposite colour or it's a red that's in tune.' It's imporant to consider the bigger picture. 'Glasses should flow. We always have full-length mirrors in our stores so that customers can step back and look at the whole silhouette.'

The *je ne sais quoi*

As with all things style-related, following your heart or your gut instinct is often the way to go. 'You should feel something, feel curious and want to try them on. Apparently there's something like 10 per cent nostalgia – the frames remind you of someone and give you a warm fuzzy feeling – and the rest of it should be new and exciting.' And when you find the perfect pair of specs, don't be afraid to make a serious investment: 'Having bespoke eyewear is a bit like having a suit made to measure: you're looking for longevity. It's an investment. Glasses can be re-polished and realigned – you can keep them forever.'

And what doesn't go

Wilkinson is not a fan of glasses on chains. 'I don't like it and it doesn't look right at any age. It's dangerous because your glasses are vulnerable.' She suggests going for varifocals instead. And, of course, the only thing worse than bad glasses is no glasses at all. 'Don't read the menu with a mobile phone light. It's more chic to have a pair of glasses.'

Great glasses brands to consider: Cutler and Gross, Oliver Peoples, Ray-Ban, Moscot, Warby Parker, Cubitts, Bailey Nelson, Eyevan, Prada.

How to wear glasses with hats

People often think that because they wear glasses, they can't wear hats. That it feels fussy and hemmed-in and there's too much going on. But there's no need to go for the full-on Audrey Hepburn in *My Fair Lady* approach. Simply avoid hats where the rim sits on the top of the glasses frame and look for simple styles that allow a bit of space. Show the face in a beret, cloche or turban. For special occasions, doff your cap to the Advanced Style set whose flamboyant outlook often involves the combination of Schiaparelli-inspired shapes and statement specs, or big hats and big glasses. After all, no one thinks twice about wearing a big floppy straw sunhat or a Stetson and sunglasses in summer, do they? As Wilkinson says, 'Glasses and hats are a yes! A wonderful opportunity for colours and shapes to play together.'

Earrings that you can wear with glasses

Small to medium hoops, studs, cuffs and diamonds – and various combinations of all of the above – go with glasses. Chandeliers? Well, Jenna Lyons does it, usually with her hair tied back. I'm not a glasses-wearer just yet (though long overdue an eye test), but I can see that the tendency is to go for a necklace or strong lips over doorknocker earrings. Keeping it sleek means less clutter around your chops and often statement glasses are enough.

Sunglasses go with everything

No longer for shady show-offs, sunglasses are an essential year-round accessory that shelter the eyes and proffer seclusion. Pick a pair that you like when you put them on. I love super-sized specs but if I wear them my small features are swamped, so I currently move between a cat's eye style bought on the cheap at Century 21 in New York and fail-safe Ray-Ban Wayfarers. Personality and mood are other considerations: for every proportion-practising Yoko Ono there's a statement-making Iris Apfel. Here are some styles you can try:

The bigger the better!

The 1970s was the decade when sunglasses expanded, when women like Natalie Wood, Donna Summer and Jackie O showed us how to go super-sized in style. Feel like having it large? Check out fashion editor Giovanna Battaglia's take on statement shades for inspiration. For maximum effect, wear hair tied back.

The iconic cateye

This style exudes old-school glamour: from 1950s Grace Kelly in a turban to Solange Knowles in Linda Farrow shades. Black frames offer timeless elegance, while tortoiseshell, embellished or coloured ones add punch to a vivid outfit.

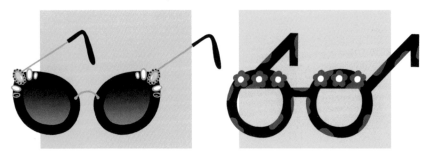

Aviators forever

See Gloria Steinem and Gwyneth Paltrow for tips on and how to wear classic metal-framed shades. And leave mirrored lenses alone.

Keep it kooky

There's a fantastic photo of Peggy Guggenheim in surrealist butterfly-shaped sunglasses that are both far-out and fabulous. These are the sunglasses to wear when you want to get noticed. See also Rihanna in vintage Chanel pearl sunglasses and Kate Hudson in Cutler and Gross' red, heart-shaped frames.

Square sunglasses

Sophia Loren wore them in the 1960s, LaDoubleJ's Viviana Volpicella wears them today. It's not that Italians do it better; it's just that wearing sunglasses has always felt like part of their DNA. It's part of everybody's now, so square up. Tip: leave hair loose to take the edge off.

Get–a–round: As Beyoncé and Linda Rodin prove, round frames look best with hair pulled back. Add a strong lipstick or big hoop earrings to complete the look.

Brands to look out for: Illesteva, Le Specs, Pomellato, Miu Miu, Céline, Linda Farrow, Karen Walker, Oliver Peoples, Moscot, Ray-Ban, Gucci, Quay Australia, Eyevan, Ellery, Prism.

No more wardrobe chaos

SORT IT OUT

In order to refresh, refine and stay current, treat your wardrobe like a celebrity treats his/her Wikipedia page and give it a constant edit. I would also recommend a bi-annual cull of clothes. Taking control of an unruly wardrobe equals a more refined personal style, a clearer vision of what to wear and less faffing around in the morning, as I found when I asked wardrobe-management expert and style consultant Anna Berkeley for advice.

Why does a fashion journalist need help sorting out her wardrobe, you might well ask. I'm not a compulsive spender or hoarder; really I'm not. Items that are no longer worn go to charity, and I do try to practise the 'one-in-one-out' rule. Having said that, I seem to have reached a plateau, I've probably achieved peak stuff (note the 'probably') and am holding onto things because they were expensive, or 'just in case'. A new tactic is needed.

When you work in fashion, you think you know it all, but it's hard to be objective about yourself. 'The difficult thing is you don't have a sounding board,' says Berkeley when I ask why we can't wardrobe-manage ourselves. 'I can do it sometimes, but then others I can't. You just end up having a round-about conversation with yourself, "I've only worn it once; it was expensive," and end up getting waylaid.' Lack of objectivity, faffing, emotional attachment, guilt; invariably there is a reason why we don't wear things. 'You need someone who is detached from all that, to talk it through with – and query it when something appears that doesn't fit in.'

Prior to the wardrobe-management session, we go through what I want to achieve (clarity, a more streamlined wardrobe), as well as more specific stuff about my age, shape and personal style.

'The more clothes you have, the harder it is to get dressed and make outfits. Ironic, but true,' points out Berkeley, and this is the catalyst I need. Some of the clothes and accessories crammed into my wardrobe have got to go. Let the fashion editor see the clothes rail.

Getting rid is surprisingly easy. No ifs, no buts, I am more than happy to see the back of a load of old clothes I never wear. Having left my job on a magazine to go freelance 12 years ago, I'm finally letting go of the 'fashion editor' clothes I've been hanging onto. 'If you're not wearing something, it's already gone,' continues Berkeley, 'and it's taking up a slot in your wardrobe that could be used for something you really love.'

Surrounded by bags of unwanted stuff (the equivalent of two large suitcases) – including a flax-coloured, summer jacket that suddenly feels very 'Jeremy Corbyn' and some boots I can't walk in – I'm on a natural decluttering high. It's such a good feeling, both cathartic and energising; I feel freer and I can't wait to drop everything off at the charity shop. All it takes is a little advice from an independent expert, someone detached from the wardrobe chaos with a clear, objective vision. And I am not going back. I am rid of the clothes from another life.

While not completely streamlined, I can now see what's what in my wardrobe – I have enough khaki shirts and jumpsuits to last a lifetime – and, currently, I don't need any more stuff. I've realised it's much better to spend time experimenting with what I already have. I don't want any new clothes; I want the space more. Now I'm getting evangelical...

The aftermath...

What's left in my cupboards is the not-so-basic basics, the wardrobe glue that holds everything together, my favourite flat shoes (brogues, sneakers and Chelsea boots), and a few showbiz pieces. These jazzy numbers are a great way to elevate the essentials: a gold-sequin biker jacket that looks ace with faded jeans and a grey-marl T-shirt, and a couple of pairs of fancy pants (gold Lurex, stretch Isabel Marant trousers; rust-and-navy brocade Jaeger party trousers). Unleashing a little liveliness into an everyday wardrobe is the perfect route to casual glamour.

'Think carefully about your unique style: is it intrinsically casual or super smart? This should guide your choices,' adds Berkeley. 'You need to be really thinking about your buying choices and not madly spending just because you want something new. Have less, not more.' In other words, dress for the lifestyle you have, not the one you wish you had. Be realistic. Stick to what suits both body shape and personality, and then add regular, carefully chosen style updates – and the odd showbiz piece that you love, to keep everything looking fresh and modern. And remember, too much stuff is just too much.

Being organised helps eliminate last-minute panic-buying and ensures that any new items purchased add mileage to existing clothes. Replace wardrobe chaos with wardrobe calm, and breathe...

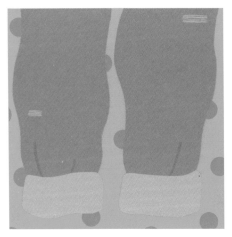
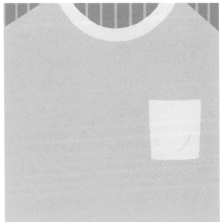

Anna Berkeley's six expert decluttering tips:

1. Do it in small chunks. Get all your tops together, rather than throwing all your clothes on the bed and running out of steam halfway through. Use a rail if you have one – it helps.

2. Try on as much as you can manage and be really honest – does it make you feel good? Does it suit you? Do you love it? You need to answer 'yes' to all of these – otherwise it's goodbye!

3. Discard anything that looks tired, fits badly or is damaged.

4. Don't save clothes for 'best' or 'just in case'. Use the things you really love – otherwise, quite frankly, what's the point?

5. Try to group your clothes into lifestyle sections – work, leisure, weekend and special occasion. This makes it easier to see what you have and to get dressed in a hurry.

6. I always advocate packing up the items you aren't wearing, so summer clothes can be packed away and replaced by winter items. Use vacuum packs to release space. And throw in some moth repellent sachets while you're at it.

FIVE QUESTIONS A PERSONAL STYLIST SHOULD ASK YOU

There are friends of mine who have had brilliant experiences with high-street personal shoppers, and then others who have had a terrible time (one who was looking for a non-wedding wedding dress and ended up in tears). I've never personally used one, so I spoke to Pandora Delevingne – aristocrat, mother to Cara, Chloe and Poppy, and former personal shopper at Selfridges.

Delevigne explains: 'First of all, I'd start with the discussion about lifestyle, shape and price range – some people can afford Prada, others can afford Topshop – to establish certain things. And I have to suss out a person's character; what we wear is a very personal thing and it depends on lifestyle. Whether you're a mother with kids or a 60-year-old on the board of a charity, the clothes have to work for you.'

The key is to start with the foundations and build from there. 'Getting the right BRA (in capital letters!) and underpinnings can do wonders,' continues Delevingne. 'Look at hair and make-up, too. I was lucky enough to work at Selfridges with experts to hand. After I'd had a make-up lesson, the difference for me was enormous. Get the basics right and you're set and running.'

A fresh eye can be really helpful. A good style consultant should listen to the client's needs and introduce them to something new. 'I go around and try to adhere to the customer's answers so that when they arrive they walk into a "Room of Dreams" – plus a few exceptions,' says Delevingne. And the customer needs to be prepared to experiment, take a risk and go for something different. 'A lot of women don't experiment enough, then they try something on and feel good in it and are amazed.'

Here are five questions a personal shopper should ask:

1. What are your main priorities during the session and what do you want to achieve?

2. Has your body or lifestyle changed recently?

3. What are the items you always wear? Or, what would you miss if it wasn't in your wardrobe?

4. How would you describe your style?

5. Are you ready for a new look or to try something new?

HOW TO WEAR THE BASICS (AND NOT LOOK BASIC)

Showstopping, showbiz items may grab all the attention but it's the versatile, flattering pieces that do all the hard work. These are the everyday essentials that go with everything, act as wardrobe glue and – if they're well-fitting – never look basic. My favourites are jeans, jackets and shirts (many items I've had for years), but do keep an eye on small but significant changes to silhouette or proportion to avoid getting stuck in a style rut. Linda Rodin has a tailor who alters her clothes to improve the fit, while Lucinda Chambers finds going on a work trip liberating because with fewer clothes she has to stretch the imagination and practise mixing and matching. Look for colour, texture and print to boost the basics and dress up your daywear.

'I don't want to think
about my clothes
when I put them on.
Feel is hugely important –
it really matters to me
and is as important as the
look. If it looks nice and
I don't feel comfortable,
I won't wear it.
I really do have to feel
right to function.'

Amy de la Haye
Dress historian, curator, author and professor at
London College of Fashion

The super shirt

I've never been able to get excited about the white shirt. It was part of my school uniform and frankly looked best after the class had signed their names all over it on the last day of term. (Remember that?) Then, as a fashion editor, the white shirt became one of the items 'every woman should own', and I didn't. Though it looks fantastic on other women, it's just not for me and blue-and-white striped for summer is the closest I get to a total whiteout. To me, the lovely blue shirt, with its complexion-enhancing properties, has always had the edge. Top of my list is always a beautiful cornflower-blue men's shirt from Margaret Howell that's several years old and looks fantastic with faded jeans. Other shirt-y stalwarts come in shades of khaki, navy blue and black and are guaranteed to remain stylish forever.

There are loads of stylish ways to wear the super shirt. Update the classics à la Emmanuelle Alt and wear a white shirt with Levi's 501s and red slingbacks. Or freshen things up by teaming a sky-blue shirt with white jeans and a denim jacket. Pale suede ankle boots with a mid heel work well with white-not-quite outfits. Go for modern military, with a khaki shirt and white culottes (or vice versa) and pointed flats; add a neckerchief to whoop things up. Perk up a navy shirt with a pair of fancy pants (printed trousers) and ballet flats. The best way to wear a white shirt is oversized on the beach, over a bikini. Or make like Patti Smith and add a black tie or bow and mussed-up hair.

Where to find the best shirts: COS, Palmer Harding, Frank & Eileen, Margaret Howell, Tome, Gap, Equipment, Alex Eagle, Bruta, Anna Quan.

The jeans you can live in

Often when I'm getting dressed, I start with a pair of jeans. Here are six silhouettes for denim lovers, plus the shoes and tops that go with them:

What goes with flared jeans?
On the top half: a denim shirt (tucked in), a figure-hugging T-shirt, a pull-on-and-go top, a roll-neck sweater, a peasant blouse, a vintage cropped, tailored jacket.
On the feet: lace-ups, brogues, sneakers, clogs, 1970s heeled ankle boots.

What goes with boyfriend jeans?
On the top half: a figure-hugging T-shirt, a military jacket, a tuxedo jacket, a Bella Freud jumper, a silk blouse, a pyjama shirt.
On the feet: hi-tops, loafers, Birkenstocks, flat sandals, heeled pumps, pointed flats, sliced loafers.

What goes with straight-leg jeans?
(I usually wear mine with a small turn-up.)
On the top half: a kimono top or belted jacket, a pussy-bow blouse, a men's shirt, a trench coat, an off-the-shoulder top, a bomber jacket.
On the feet: Chelsea boots, sneakers, hi-tops, heeled ankle boots, platforms/flatforms.

What goes with skinny jeans?

On the top half: a blazer and T-shirt, a voluminous top, a tunic, a cocoon coat, a boyfriend jacket.

On the feet: heeled ankle boots, lace-ups, brogues, flatforms, kitten heels, slingbacks, pointed flats, ballet pumps.

Denim disciples love: Frame, Levi's, Uniqlo, J Brand, J.Crew, Re/Done, Rag & Bone, A.P.C., Mother Denim, AG Jeans, Gap, Paige, M.i.h., Sass & Bide, Topshop.

What goes with bootcut jeans?

On the top half: a super shirt, a long-sleeved T-shirt (tucked in) and a skinny scarf, a roll-neck sweater, a silk blouse, a denim jacket, a Chanel-style tweed jacket, a blazer.

On the feet: boots (of course), babouche slippers, pointed flat slingbacks.

What goes with cropped flared jeans?

On the top half: a denim jacket, a Breton top, a biker jacket, a tunic or shirtdress, a duster coat, a cotton shirt.

On the feet: heeled 1970s-style ankle boots, mid-heel pumps, pointed flats, slingbacks, plimsolls, Gucci loafers.

The pull-on-and-go top

Most of the time I'm in jeans and having a portfolio career means there's a sliding scale of smartness. On the days when I'm working from home, I'm more thrown-together, but I'll often have to nip out to a quick meeting or event – and this is where the pull-on-and-go top comes in. It's the hot-weather version of the blazer over a T-shirt and smart enough to pass muster with jeans, loafers and a scarf. In winter, this wardrobe basic becomes an above-the-table, dinner-party top with pattern, embroidery or print that engages guests and perks up the proceedings.

Where to go for pull-on-and-go: Joie, Boden, Marni, Velvet by Graham & Spencer, Jigsaw, Dries van Noten, Cédric Charlier, Ellery, Matin Studio, Sacai.

Run-around pants
(how leggings have changed)

When I was first asked to write about leggings for the *Guardian*, I thought the fashion team had lost the plot. But then I realised that leggings in substantial fabrics are more like stretch trousers than footless tights, and this is what women wear today, particularly in winter with a big coat, black ankle boots or sneakers. 'People are very busy, so clothes have to work even harder,' says Donna Ida Thornton, CEO of the Donna Ida boutiques and online store. 'I have a pair of black J Brand leather leggings that are the hardest working item in my wardrobe. They've never been cleaned or washed and they work all year round.'

Where to buy the best leggings: Hey Jo,
J Brand, hush, Joseph, Winser London, Hobbs,
Country Road.

Ways to
wear leggings

Try wearing them with an oversized white shirt and a neat black jumper over the top. Then add a simple black pump or skate shoe for running around in. 'Leather leggings can look slightly sexy, so style them down with a chunky knit or a classic blazer and white T-shirt,' advises Thornton. Or team leggings with a cocoon coat or a sleeveless gilet dress and brogues. Remember, leggings come in a range of colours, so forget black and think about navy, forest green and wine-coloured ones, too. Try a duster coat over leggings in tonal colours.

Don't go too dressy. You need a contrast, not two slippery fabrics together. Leather leggings and a silky blouse can feel a bit Jackie Collins. And beware of flimsy fabrics that are so thin you can see your underwear through them – no-one wants that.

The statement skirt

The only skirt I ever wear is a maxi skirt. In summer, I break out an indigo jersey version from J.Crew that goes perfectly with a navy silk V-neck top from Winser London. This is one of those winning combinations that looks like a very chic maxi dress and can take me from a business meeting to a rooftop bar and beyond. My other maxi skirt is a black sequined number bought in the M&S sale and worn on my 50th birthday with a blush-pink silk blouse from Diane von Furstenberg and silver Roger Vivier flats. It was freezing in New York on New Year's Eve, but this marvellous maxi skirt is a perfectly glamorous way to keep your legs warm when hailing a yellow cab.

Fans of knee-length or midi styles can practise the art of mismatch (contrasting textures or genres adds oomph) by pairing a metallic sunray pleat, the patterned or sequined pencil and the brocade or corduroy A-line with a cashmere sweater, grey sweatshirt or super shirt.

Where to shop for skirts: Whistles, Diane von Fürstenberg, Le Kilt, Boden, Sonia Rykiel, The Row, Zara, Baum und Pferdgarten, By Johnny, LK Bennett.

The pull-it-together piece (a kick-ass jacket)

For a very special occasion (all right, it was for the launch party of my first book *Style Forever*), I had a blowout on a Céline tuxedo jacket. Ordinarily, I baulk at spending more than a certain amount on an item of clothing (over £200 and I feel sick for days) and this was the most I'd ever splurged. But quality counts. And I knew investing in *le smoking* was the right thing to do, so there was no buyer's remorse.

This once-in-a-lifetime jacket looked the business; I felt confident and chic and made an understated style statement in jeans and a T-shirt and my pull-it-together piece. Job done.

Good tailoring is a smart way to add gravitas to any outfit. I'll have the Céline tuxedo jacket for the rest of my life (as long as the moths don't get greedy). The superpower jacket also goes with black coated jeans, capri pants, or a pair of stretchy black-and-gold Lurex pants. I've worn it over a jumpsuit, with boyfriend jeans and one day might even do an 'Olsen Twins' and team a masculine jacket with an evening dress. Perhaps I'll save that for my next book launch...

Jackets that don't all cost a packet: Jigsaw, ME+EM, J.Crew, Massimo Alba, Zara.

The outstanding coat

Last winter I discovered the allure of the go-anywhere cocoon coat. Perfect for layering over jackets and jeans and roomy enough to wear on my bicycle.

The outstanding coat is another fabulous pull-it-together piece that can sharpen the most casual silhouette. Think about figure-flattering cuts and colours that suit a wintry complexion, as well as warmth, wear and longevity. No need to binge buy, but you will need more than one... Here are 10 outstanding coats and how to wear them.

1. The classic mac: Go for Katharine Hepburn's under-the-radar glamour. Arriving at Idlewild Airport (now JFK) in 1956, Hepburn wore a stone-coloured mac, big scarf, flared chinos and flat, black, buckled leather shoes. An eternally chic ensemble. See Margaret Howell for the modern-day equivalent.

2. The military coat doesn't have to stand to attention: French model and music producer Caroline de Maigret uses a black jumper, jeans and hi-top sneakers to give hers a laidback vibe. For a softer spin, juxtapose a khaki coat with a floral-print silk dress.

3. Faux fur or shaggy sheepskin: In 1964, model Jean Shrimpton was photographed by then-boyfriend David Bailey for *Vogue*. The Shrimp looked stunning in a plum Mongolian lamb coat and patent-leather boots. Totally timeless.

4. The great cape: OK, they're a bit fiddly for everyday (if you want to actually use your arms or carry a bag), but capes can look great for evening. Julianne Moore proved as much by wearing one over a slinky Armani floor-length gown on the red carpet. Those not attending the Oscars can go for the cape-over-cocktail-dress option.

5. Gorgeous graphics always look good: From Josephine Baker in a striped 1920s dress suit to Rosita Missoni in a zigzag coatigan today; a bold, graphic, single-breasted style makes a striking statement.

6. The cocoon coat: Garance Doré looks perfect in a primrose-yellow oversized Stella McCartney overcoat. White jeans are rolled up and shoes are soft, black leather, pointed, run-around flats. Just add a grey cashmere scarf, sunglasses and a cup of Joe.

7. Leopard print forever: In the 1960s, Catherine Deneuve wore hers with a mini dress and black leather slingbacks, and she's often seen on the front row in leopard print and black pants and a sweater today. A strong red accent (lipstick and leather handbag) seals the look.

8. The trench coat: At Paris Fashion Week, 2015, Charlotte Rampling rocked up in a belted suede trench, clear Perspex sunglasses and an elegant black dress, 20-denier tights (pantyhose) and black, heeled lace-ups. Chic as you like.

9. The belted wrap coat: Croon along with Diane Keaton in 'You Don't Own Me' at the end of *The First Wives Club* – then hit the street in a beautiful, belted wool coat.

10. Brightly coloured and vintage-inspired: Diana Vreeland's 'pink is the navy blue of India' comment was sparked by a pink mohair edge-to-edge Jaeger coat (in a photograph by Norman Parkinson of the model Anne Gunning in Jaipur in 1956). This kind of standout coat never goes out of style.

Where to find an outstanding coat: COS, Harris Wharf, Ganni, Max Mara, Jaeger, Jigsaw, Burberry, Mackintosh, Raey, Han Studios.

NAVAZ BATLIWALLA

'There comes a point when you have something of a uniform and when you get there it becomes a lot easier because you can just replenish staple pieces. But it's important to add personality to these failsafe wardrobe basics and, of course, to look modern. I wear classic flat-front boy pants (from Joseph) in cobalt blue or fuchsia, with Church's brogues and an oversized charcoal sweater. In the summer, faded pink or green chinos do the trick, with a Breton for timeless Mediterranean charm. A workaday tote in grained Kelly green leather is another way to bring a neutral outfit to life, accompanied by a men's gold watch or simple jewellery. And a short red manicure (I like Chanel's 'Pirate') or a red lip to amp up white or navy is always a winner.

What I do pay attention to are tone and texture. For head-to-toe black or navy, texture becomes important in adding interest. A cashmere cable knit layered over a silk blouse worn with rigid Japanese denim looks more considered than head-to-toe jersey and doesn't take that much more effort.

My 'grown-up tomboy' style is rooted in quality pieces that don't date. I have been dressing this way since the early 1990s, which was when this androgynous look really came into its own. The designers of that time – Helmut Lang, Ann Demeulemeester, A.P.C. and Jil Sander – created clothes that looked effortless, were superbly cut and just fitted my shape. Obviously I would also buy the high-street versions of those cuts on my first-jobber salary.

I love to have a cropped ankle (it's all about trousers; I rarely wear skirts or dresses) or bracelet sleeves. I'm very particular about details, so armholes, necklines and waists have to sit in the right place. I do also like some oversized boyfriend silhouettes but I have to be careful as I'm very slight, just 5 ft 3 in (1.6 m).'

Stylist, journalist and creative consultant

ELIMINATE FAFFAGE AND THROW IT IN THE FASHION BIN

There are some fashion items that are about as much use as the England football team during a penalty shoot-out. Simplify your life by steering clear of the following:

Clutch bags

As a fan of faff-free style, one thing you will never see me with is a clutch. I tried one once and it's a miracle I even got to the event without losing the clutch bag, my travel card and my marbles. And once there, I felt clumsy and kept spilling my drink – who needs that? Release the clutch...

Over-the-knee boots

As worn by Dick Whittington, Julia Roberts in *Pretty Woman* and Kim Kardashian – take your pick. No, don't.

The off-the shoulder top

Or anything else that requires 'special' underwear. I tried the off-the-shoulder top, so that you don't have to. Looks lovely in photos, needs frequent readjustment to stay in place and hence, does not work in real life. Pure faffage. The same applies to clingy, skimpy dresses that can only be worn with shapewear. Sling the Spanx – there are other ways to look good.

High heels

Chapter 4, Flat Shoes Forever (see page 88).

Cut-out swimsuits or dresses
As far as I'm concerned, there's nothing sharp about looking like a paparazzi-friendly Z-lister on a fake beach in Dubai. Cut-out clothing is complicated, fiddly and crass. Forget about it.

Clothes made from polyester or acrylic
Even if they are Comme des Garçons. I'm surprised that manufacturers still use these fabrics to make anything other than sportswear. No one benefits from hot-flush-inducing clothes or Van de Graff Generator-style hair.

Thongs and C-strings
Did anyone, ever feel comfortable with a string of fabric or, even worse, a bit of wire covered with fabric (the C-string) stuck between their bum cheeks? Of course not. Big pants are best or, if needs must, do a Dame Vivienne Westwood and go commando.

Hobble skirts, corsets and anything that might appear at a historical re-enactment
It's not the 19th century, people.

Pool slides
Ignore any fashion article telling you that pool slides are 'the shoe of the summer'. These revolting plastic sandals should not be worn outside a leisure facility, health spa or mental institution – and never, ever teamed with athletic socks. Just say no.

Jeans with ready-made rips
Natural wear and tear is perfectly fine. But fake ripped knees are like fake news: best ignored.

'Style is never dictated by ephemeral trends. It's an air of ease and individuality. Style is wearing it well; the clothes never overpower the wearer. It's not costume-y. Moreover, it's not defined as the ability to afford and purchase the most expensive designer clothing. That's just being rich!'

Claudette Prosper
Fashion journalist and stylist

ALYSON WALSH

Described by the *Daily Telegraph* as one of the 'women over 40 influencing the internet', Alyson Walsh is a freelance fashion journalist, author and founder of the popular blog *That's Not My Age*. A former fashion editor with many years experience on women's magazines, she now writes for the *Financial Times* and the *Guardian*. Alyson's first book, *Style Forever*, was published in 2015.

Acknowledgements

To all the brilliant women I interviewed for this book, thank you for your time and for your remarkable expertise. Thanks to Kate and Kajal at Hardie Grant and to Ayumi for the fantastic illustrations. Thank you to Mary for the beautiful design. To my lovely friend Hat Margolies for providing office space and a desk to work from when the builders arrived halfway through chapter two (you're stuck with me now, I'm staying). Thanks as always to Emma Marsden for all the coffee, expert advice and encouragement – basically for being a lifelong friend and 'Book Coach'. Thanks to Adrienne Wyper for expert proofreading when you really had better things to do. To Navaz Batliwalla for perennial Net Nannying, and more. To Katherine Boxall at UCA for her superstar support. Thank you to Vicci Bentley and Elaine Kingett for contributing to *That's Not My Age* and being ace. Lydia Patyra for helping out behind the scenes, and Angie Somerside for her expert design eye. But most of all to my beloved Paul (Mr That's Not My Age); you're an angel and I really would be feral without you.

Know Your Style by Alyson Walsh

First published in 2017 by Hardie Grant Books

Hardie Grant Books (UK)
52-54 Southwark Street
London SE1 1UN
hardiegrant.com

Hardie Grant Books (Australia)
Ground Floor, Building 1
658 Church Street
Melbourne, VIC 3121
hardiegrant.com

British Library Cataloguing-in-Publication Data. A catalogue record
for this book is available from the British Library.

ISBN: 978-1-78488-118-4

Publisher: Kate Pollard
Senior Editor: Kajal Mistry
Editorial Assistant: Hannah Roberts
Publishing Assistant: Eila Purvis
Art Direction: Mary Lees
Illustrations © Ayumi Takahashi
Author photo on page 158 © Annie Johnston
Copy editor: Victoria Lyle
Proofreader: Kate Truman
Colour Reproduction by p2d

Printed and bound in China by 1010

10 9 8 7 6 5 4 3 2 1